M000102211

Letters from
Wyoming Territory:
1870-1879

Check out Kent Brooks other titles available at

Amazon.com &

Lonesomeprairie.com:

Old Boston: As Wild As They Come

Letters from Colorado: 1880-1889

Letters from Wyoming: 1880-1889

Letters from Nebraska: 1880-1889

Letters from Indian Territory: 1880-1888

Cattle & Cowboys: Letters & More from the 1880s

Letters from Wyoming 1870-1879

Letters from Wyoming Territory: 1870-1879

The Heading West Series

Compiled and Annotated

By

Kent Brooks
&
Colin Brooks

Kent Brooks
2019

All rights reserved. This book or any portion thereof may not be reproduced or used in any manner whatsoever without the express written permission of the publisher except for the use of brief quotations in a book review or scholarly journal.

First Printing: 2019

ISBN 9781091150577

Lonesome Prairie Publications
PO Box 842
Casper, WY 82601

www.lonesomeprairie.com

Ordering Information:

Special discounts are available on quantity purchases by corporations, associations, educators, and others. For details, contact the publisher at the above listed address.

Dedication

To the hardy pioneers of old who traveled on foot, on horses, in wagons, via rail and any other means they could to settle the American West. Through the "pen pictures" painted in these letters, you get an unfiltered, first-person account of what they saw when they came to this new place.

Contents

Acknowledgements

The idea and initial content for this work originate from the research I did for my book, "Old Boston: As Wild As They Come." Thanks to the historians of old who didn't have access to the resources available today. I appreciate their work more than ever. I can't imagine putting this project together with a typewriter and without access to digital archives which are available today.

Thank you, God, in heaven for the ability to work. With my brother, who had cerebral palsy, in mind, not everyone gets that gift. I am humbled to have the opportunity to work on compiling this small piece of history about those who came before us.

As I worked on my book *"Old Boston: As Wild As They Come"* I found myself enthralled with the news of yesteryear and with the writing of frontier newspapermen of the 1880s. The more I read these old-time newspapers, the more I wanted to learn. When searching for information about Boston, Colorado, I found connections to various states and territories including the area which is now the state of Wyoming. This discovery started my search for more information.

This compilation of letters, reports, and telegrams is from individuals and correspondents about places they came to visit and things they saw during this time. Although the focus is on the letters, I have added a few other newspaper artifacts such as advertisements and short news clippings to provide additional detail and context to era.

There are letters from people who came west for their health, from those who were exploring and seeking their fortune and from those who were hiding from something in their past. These brave individuals; men, women, young and old; took to heart the phrase often attributed to Horace Greeley,

"Go west young man, go west and grow up with the country."

The letters compiled for this project tell of life in those days, sometimes good and sometimes not so good. Besides the good news and the wonder people had about the American West, you will sometimes find tragedy. I present content in the following order:

- Each chapter begins with one of my favorite quotes from that year.
- For each letter you will see:
  - The header for the message is as they presented it in the old-time newspaper.
  - The paper in which they published the letter is listed, so you will know where the writer was from (there are exceptions).
  - The text from the letter. They often addressed it to the editor of the paper.
  - Commentary, if I have any or if it relates to a separate project. Sometimes I present foot-notes to support understanding of the content. I sometimes use footnotes to clarify abbreviations or locations.

There are also many alternate spellings and slang terms in old newspapers that may or may not have meaning. They often spell canyon, "canon." The term cozy is spelled "cosy." Stayed is often spelled "staid." Boulder is often spelled "Bowlder. With this work you must assume that is the way they wrote it in the 1880s. Other things you will see include the use of the term Ultimo or ult. This refers to the previous month. A December newspaper which says "12th ult." is referring to November 12th. The term "&c." is often used in place of "etc."

There are many variations of terms and abbreviations and spellings which are in error by modern standards. Understanding this will help with your enjoyment of this material. I hope you enjoy these letters as much as I have.

These writings are part of the nostalgia of the old days and for which we sometimes long. Newspapers of the early days are a great way to learn more about those times. People were interested in the west as shown by the following excerpt:

> *Having an hour's leisure, I thought I would drop a line, in the hope that I may receive a long letter from you, giving me an account of the progress of the good people of Jackson county.*
> -Letter from Wyoming Territory, 1873.

> *Having had more requests to write to my friends of Gibson and vicinity than will be possible for me to comply with, I thought would avail myself of the kindly offered privilege of your columns.*
> -Letter from Wyoming Territory, 1873.

Often local newspapers were exchanged with other publications from places where settlers had moved. Those newspapers in the hometowns would then share with the community bits and pieces of the lives of former citizens. Those tidbits include reports of people traveling to engage in new vocations, marriage notices, deaths, and obits, murders, fights and shootings, legal notices, prices for commodities and more.

There was always some news sent home of interesting happenings in the area in which someone had previously resided. Letters sent "home" often explained with wonder a new place a person was visiting or was moving. For me there has been no better way to retrace the steps of those who traveled west in the 1800s. Through various letters written to the folks back home or to others for multiple purposes, political or otherwise, we will look further into the soul of the early days of Wyoming before it was a state. This compilation differs from the other books in the letters series as it covers only 1880-1888.

Thanks for taking the time to read and I hope you enjoy reading this history as much as I have.

Chapter 1: 1870

The scenery between the Fort (Laramie) and Chugstation is very grand line of bluffs rising ninety to one hundred and fifty feet in height running for miles, broken up by passages between, look like some old castle of medieval times, crumbling into ruins.

-Letter from Wyoming Territory, 1870.

WOMAN'S RIGHT TO VOTE.—The following is the text of the bill granting women the right to vote, which has lately become a law in the territory of Wyoming: A bill "for an act to grant to the women of Wyoming Territory the right of suffrage, and to hold office." Be it enacted, &c.

Sec. 1. That every woman of the age of twenty-one years, residing in this Territory, may at every election to be holden under the laws thereof, cast her vote. And her rights to the elective franchise and to hold office shall be the same under the election laws of the Territory as those of electors.

Sec. 2. This act shall take effect and be in force from and after its passage.

A private letter from Wyoming says: "Now send along your superfluous women!" which is as much as to say that the act was passed for the especial purpose of enticing the ladies to the Territory.

The *South-Western* (Shreveport, Louisiana) 5 Jan 1870.
The *Clarion-Ledger* (Jackson, Mississippi) 1 Jan 1870.

A Cheyenne letter says : "Mayor Burt recently got from a Crow Chief a spicula of gold, as long as a lead pencil, and half as thick as his finger. The Indians would never reveal where they got their gold, but said there was plenty of it."

Quad-City Times **(Davenport, Iowa) 2 Feb 1870.**

THE GAZETTE.

WOMAN JURORS IN WYOMING.

Letter from Judge Howe.

From the Chicago Legal News, April 9.

Janesville Daily Gazette **(Janesville Wisconsin) 12 Apr 1870.** — We have from the first taken great interest in the experiment in Wyoming, of allowing juries to be composed of both men and women, as we saw many contradictory statements in regard to the Wyoming juries going the rounds of the press, we wrote to the Hon. J. H. Howe, Chief Justice of the Supreme Court of that Territory, requesting him to give us his views as to the success of the experiment. We are pleased to publish the letter of Judge Howe, which is all the most sanguine friend of the cause could desire. The Judge, after writing the letter upon request, consented to its publication as written:

"CHEYENNE, WYOMING, April 4, 1870.

"Mrs. Myra Bradwell, Chicago, Ill,:

[1]"DEAR MADAM: I am in receipt of your favor of the 26th ult., in which you request me to give you a truthful statement, over my own signature, for publication in your paper, of the history of, and my observation in regard to, the woman grand and petit jurors of Wyoming. I will comply with your request, with this qualification, that it be not published over my own signature, as I do not covet newspaper publicity, and have already, without any agency or fault of my own been subjected to an amount of it which I never anticipation or conceived of, and which has been far from agreeable to me.

"I had not agency in the enactment of the law in Wyoming conferring legal equality upon women. I found it upon the statue book of that Territory, and in accordance with its provisions several women were legally drawn by the proper officers on the grand and petit juries of Albany County, and were duly summoned by the Sheriff without any agency of mine. On being apprised of these facts, I conceived it to be my plain duty to fairly enforce this is my law, as I would any other; and more than this, I resolved at once that, as it had fallen to my lot to have the experiment tried under my administration, it should have a fair trial, and I therefore assured these women that they could serve or not, as they chose; that if they chose to serve, the Court would secure to them the most respectful consideration and deference, and protect them from insult in word or gesture, and from anything

---

[1] NOTE: This letter had open quotation marks at the points shown, but no closing quotation marks.

7

which might offend a modest and virtuous woman in any of the walks of life in which the good and true women of our country have been accustomed to move.

"While I have never been an advocate for the law, I felt that thousands of good men and women had been, and that they had a right to see it fairly administered; and I resolved that it should not be, sneered down if I had to employ the whole power of the court to prevent it. It felt even those who were opposed to the policy of admitting women to the right of suffrage and to hold office would condemn me if I did not do this. It was also sufficient for me that my own judgement approved this.

With such assurances, these women chose to serve, and were duly impaneled as jurors. They are educated, cultivated Eastern ladies, who are an honor to their sex. They have, true womanly devotion, left their homes of comfort in the States, to share the fortunes of their husbands and brothers in the far West, and to aid them in founding a new State beyond the Missouri.

And now as to the results. With all my prejudices against the policy, I am under conscientious obligations to say that these women acquitted themselves with such dignity, decorum, propriety of conduct, and intelligence as to win the admiration of every fair mined citizen of Wyoming. They were careful, painstaking, intelligent and conscientious. They were firm and resolute for the rights as established by the law and testimony. Their verdicts were right, and after three or four criminal trials, the lawyers engaged in the defending persons accused of crime began to avail themselves of the right of peremptory challenge to get rid of the woman jurors, who were too much in favor of enforcing the laws and punishing crime to suit the interests of their clients! After the grand jury had been in session two days, the dance-house keepers, gamblers, and *demi-monde* fled out of the city in dismay, to escape the indictment of women grand jurors! In short, I have never, in twenty-five years of constant experience in the courts of the country, seen a more faithful, intelligent, and resolutely honest grand and petit jury than these.

A contemptibly lying and silly dispatch went over the wires to the effect that during the trial of A. W. Howie for homicide in which the jury consisting of six women and six men, the men and women were kept locked up together all night for four nights. Only two nights intervened during the trial, and on these nights, by my order, the jury were taken to the parlor of the large, commodious and well-furnished hotel of the Union Pacific Railroad, in charge of the Sheriff and a woman bailiff, where they were supplied with meals and every comfort, and at 10 o'clock the women were conducted by the bailiff to a large and suitable apartment, where beds were prepared for them, and the men to another adjoining, were beds were prepared for them, and where they remained in charge of sworn officers until morning, when they were again all conducted to the parlor and from thence in a body to breakfast, and thence to the jury room, which was a clean and comfortable one, carpeted and heated, and furnished with all proper conveniences.

The cause was submitted to the jury for their decision about 11 o'clock in the forenoon, and they agreed upon their verdict, which was received by the court between 11 and 12 o'clock at night of the same day, when they were discharged.

Everybody commended the conduct of this jury, and were satisfied with their verdict, except the individual who was convicted of murder in the second degree.

The presence of these ladies in court secured the most perfect decorum and propriety of conduct, and the gentlemen of the bar and others vied with each other in their courteous and respectful demeanor toward the ladies and the court. Nothing occurred to offend the most refined lady (if she was a sensible lady), and the universal judgement of every intelligent and fair minded man present, was and is, that the experiment was a success.

I dislike the notoriety this matter has given me, but do not shrink from it. I never sought it nor expected it. And have only performed what I regarded as a plain duty, neither seeking nor desiring any praise, and quite indifferent to any censure or criticism which my conduct may have invoked.

Thank you for your friendly and complimentary expressions. I am very respectfully, yours. **J. H. HOWE.**

LETTER FROM WYOMING.

ATLANTIC CITY, WYOMING TERRITORY, ⎰
May 14th, 1870, ⎱

Janesville Daily Gazette (Janesville, Wisconsin) 23 May 1870. —
Editors Gazette: Hearing; various reports from Wisconsin in regard to
this place, and the raids of the Indians, I wish to State through the Gazette a few facts. Having arrived here from Albion, Wis. only some
three weeks since, I know but little of the early history, yet I learn that
on the 20th of March the Sioux Indians made a raid on this place, killing seven men and running off some horses and mules, but did not
enter the village. One man was killed within three fourths of a mile of
town, that being the nearest they came. Again on the 4th inst.,[2] they
made another raid about daylight, but were unsuccessful, there being
a company of the U.S. Cavalry camped within a mile and a half, that
the Indians were not aware of, under the command of Major Gordon,
that went in pursuit in squads of from five to ten, retaking what stock
they had started, skirmishing nearly all day, killing, it is supposed
seven Indians, losing one Lieutenant and one Sargent, shot through
the jaws breaking them both. Last night's reports say he is gaining
slowly. Day before yesterday another company of cavalry came to re-
inforce those here, so we feel comparatively safe. This seems to be
the base of the Indian depredations, there being more stock here than

---

[2] Reminder "inst." is a reference of time. It is an abbreviation for
instante mense, meaning a date of the current month, such as "the 4th
inst." or 4th of this month.

at other points. Obtaining stock seems to be their main object, altho'
if they find a man out alone they are apt to take his scalp.

Reports from Ft. Bridger, last night, claim the Bunnies and
Snakes, hitherto peaceable, passing through this place on the 12th inst.
Are now on the war path. Owing to the failure of the Indian Agents
to meet them at three different times set for them to receive their annuities, they have taken up the war whoop, determined on revenge;
but reports may prove it different.

There is a great, deal of complaint about those entrusted with Indian affairs that are not acting in accordance with Government orders,
even in some cases using the money appropriated for annuities to their
own private interest and letting the Indians suffer for the want of it.
The Indians are not blamed by the settlers as the Agents are, for not
fulfilling their duty to them.

Of the country in general, mining &c., I will not speak of at present.   **Yours Truly**   **V.E NICHOLS**

Letter From Wyoming.
FORT LARAMIE, WYOMING TERR. }
July 7th, 1870. }

The Titusville Herald, **18 Jul 1870**. — Editors Morning Herald: In
your valuable paper I seldom see communications from the "Far
West," so I will try and give you a little news now and then from this
vicinity, if it will be of service to you. I suppose your readers know

Fort Laramie is situated on the Laramie River about two miles from the junction with the Platte. It was established as a trading post and was, before the completion of the railroad, the chief post on the California road. However, now it is of little importance. The late visit of Red Cloud and his warriors to Washington and various speeches and articles published in regard to them have been read by the knowing ones with disgust. To know all one should see both sides of the picture. Red Cloud and his band is no more than a band of marauding stock stealing vagabonds, robbing trains and mail parties at every opportunity, killing and frightfully mutilating every white man who crosses their path. There are cases of men being wounded while on duty at various parts of the road between Fort Fetterman here and Cheyenne. Since his (Red Cloud's) arrival here from Washington, he and his whole tribe have been lying around the fort procuring rations and ammunition for (as we all believe with good reason) a vigorous campaign. We have those among us who cry peace at any cost, but they are the ones holding fat contracts for Indian goods and those who are making money off of Indian trading. I am in favor of General Sheridan's policy of *extermination*. John Rieshaw, the half breed interpreter who accompanied Red Cloud to Washington, after shooting corporal of Company "E" 4th Infantry at Fort Fetterman in cold blood, is now allowed to go free, because it was Red Cloud's request. I regard the half breeds as more treacherous and of a more dangerous character than the Indians themselves. The garrison consists of Company's D, F and K, 4th U.S. Infantry commanding officer, Brevet

Brig. Gen. F. F. Flint, Col 4th Infantry. This is the headquarters of the Fourth Infantry and its excellent band under the leadership Prof. J. Leary. If there should be any news of any importance I will give it to you in detail as soon as possible. "Frontier."

CHEYENNE.
The Big Horn Expedition—Another Indian Outrage.

CHEYENNE, WY. T., July 29.—The *Leader* publishes a letter to-day from a member of the Big Horn expedition, dated near Gray Bull River Gully, the 19th, five hundred miles from Cheyenne. The letter says that they have not gone on the reservation, nor do they intend doing so. All are well, and they are just commencing to prospect. Mr. H. M. Plumb, who has just returned from the Bear River mines, reports finding the bodies of three more white men, killed by the Indians, in the North Park. The bodies were identified as those of Joseph Breem, Frank Marion and old man Scott, all trappers. It is the settled opinion of the best informed that the Utes are responsible for these murders.

Detroit Free Press (Detroit, Michigan) 30 Jul 1870.

Letter from Wyoming.
PORT LARAMIE, August 4th 1870

The Titusville Herald (Titusville, Pennsylvania) Aug 22, 1870. —
Editors *Morning Herald*: Were you ever in Cheyenne? You may have
been but not lately I think. Well it is at present time the most tumbled
down affair you ever saw. I had occasion to go there the other day in
mail escort and with difficulty found the town hid as it was with three
years collection of rubbish the houses are mostly frame and adobe
brick, (pronounced "doby") which are a mixture of clay and straw
made into bricks 14 by 8 inches, sun dried they make very comfortable houses but not very durable. In the center of the streets was a
miscellaneous collection of tin cans, old boots, broken crockery, bar-
rels, etc. enough to choke up the road. I was informed by a bystander
that the city authorities were discussing with becoming gravity the
question, to clean the streets or move the town.

Vice and filth go hand in hand, keno and furo are played
openly and advertised on the street corners by flaming posters.
Nearly everyone plays and the game goes on without the least check,
(except the want of stumps). Prostitutes parade the streets at all times
of day and night flaunting their gay dresses and smiling and leering as
only that class can do.

There are some traces of prosperity and more of decay in this
wonderful city. It came up as it were, in a night and had its turn of
usefulness and is now as fast going to decay. The only structures of

15

any importance are the U P R R machine shops, which are well built and have very substantial appearance.

Fort Daniel A. Russell is about three miles from the town, which is a company post. The garrison consists of five companies of the 5th cavalry and II company of the 9th Infantry. The post is commanded by Brevet Major General King Contend, 9th Infantry, and is headquarters of that regime it. Cullin's camp is situated half way between the post and town and is the depot headquarters for this portion of the frontiers.

The trip between here and Cheyenne occupies two days — the first day to Chugstation, where are stationed a detachment of the 4th infantry and a detachment of the 5th cavalry. The next day we arrive in Cheyenne about 4 pm.

The scenery between the Fort (Laramie) and Chugstation is a very grand line of bluffs rising ninety to one hundred and fifty feet in height running for miles, broken up by passages between, look like some old castle of medieval times, crumbling into ruins. The rest of the route is flat and uninteresting. The mule is accompanied by an escort of a corporal and two privates.

There is no reliable news regarding Red Cloud. Some say he is coming in to make peace, others think not.

The Big Horn expedition have all heard from the party of Indians that their supplies are giving out and they must have food soon or give up as a bad job.

There are the usual number of rascally half breeds and Indians hanging around the post during the day. At night they leave for their 'Tepee' (Sioux for house) which is composed of a dozen stout poles tied at the top with strips of buffalo hide and set up in the form of a cone. They are covered with buffalo hides, an opening at the bottom for entrance and a small one at the top for ventilation. In the morning they come back on ponies or mules and some on horses, sometimes two or three on one animal. The squaws not having been accustomed to the luxury of the side saddle do not ride sideways but otherwise. The squaws have a weakness for paint and in that respect are like their whiteface sisters only they do not show as good taste in application. They are considered to be in the height of fashion with their faces and part of their hair daubed profusely with Chinese vermeil on. They may be found at any time around the company mess houses and the sutler[3] store, waiting to receive all that may be offered or that they can make away with. It is astonishing to see what a quantity of food one of them will get away with. I fed one old fellow til I thought he burst, and still he was not satisfied. If a platter full of baked beans, two of bread and a quart of Irish stew would not satisfy him what more could I do? They evidently have a "sweet tooth" as they will trade anything they possess for a little sugar.

The paymaster (Major Burbank) made his appearance on his bi-monthly visit to pay the garrison on the 27th ultimo, the most of the

---

[3] A sutler is a person who followed an army and sold provisions to the soldiers.

money went to the sutlers for red eye, and the consequences are a number of cases in hospital broken heads, black eyes, and twelve cases for court martial. Besides there are a number carrying logs weighing from twenty to thirty pounds, from fifteen to thirty days for various offences.

You may think this a very immoral post, not thinking at all, nothing more than any other post I have served at posts east and west, I see no difference.

Whiskey is the soldiers curse, a soldier who does not drink is a *rara avis,* and if he does not on entering the army his good principles are soon overcome and he sinks to the level of his associates. It is whiskey that leads men to do most, if not all, that gets them into trouble, and in consequence drink to their own misery, but that fascination of the cup covers it and they cure their ill luck and drink deeper.

I wonder if those kind ladies of the Christian Commission have any idea that their work is all felt in the army yet it is and are remembered too with grateful feelings by many a poor sick soldier.

I found among the supplies of the Post Hospital at this place, a roll of lint with the inscription from the ladies of Crawford county Pa. written on it. I find also, bandages, pillows, and various other articles with the Christian Commission stamp upon them showing that the great work of four years is still felt although the impulse that brought into life has ceased. We cannot complete the good the U.S. Christian Commission has done, and is still doing, though it is no more.

A letter from Wyoming Station says a party of twelve whites were attacked sixty miles northwest of Bitter Creek by Indians and driven into the mountains. Two of the party are missing; three others were seriously wounded, though not fatally.

C. Penrose and S. . Merkel are the names of the men captured.

Chicago Tribune (Chicago, Illinois) 9 Aug 1870.
Detroit Free Press (Detroit, Michigan) 9 Aug 1870.

A letter from Wyoming, speaking of the election, says: "There were no sneers, no profanity, no fighting. The women went to the polls as quietly as if they were going to church. They seemed to be conscientious as to what candidates were worthy of their suffrage, many refusing to vote for men on account of intemperance."

The *Fair Haven Journal* (Fair Haven, Vermont) 24 Sep 1870.

19

It is stated in a letter from Wyoming Territory, that the combined warriors of the Sioux and Cheyennes are on the war path to attack the Shoshones, a sort of goose head tribe who are out on their fall hunt. Arrangements were on foot by the United States troops to protect the Shoshones.

Atchison Daily Patriot (Atchison, Kansas) 29 Oct 1870.

Our climate is delightful, scenery beautiful (that no poet can deny) and nature when in her more propitious mood presents varied charms to the painter, hunter, the mineralogist, the lover of piscatory and aquatic sports, and I am the philosopher who could find many pleasant walks without fear of stumbling over his patron rock.

-Letter from Wyoming Territory, 1871.

Letter from Wyoming Territory.

RAWLINGS SPRINGS, WY.,
Dec. 26, 1870.

Editors Morning Herald:

The Titusville Herald (Titusville, Pennsylvania) · 2 Jan 1871. — From the fact that quite a large number of Pennsylvanians are resident in Wyoming, I have no doubt but a few observations in relation to this country will interesting to your readers.

THE NEW TERRITORY

named I believe, in honor of one of the counties in the old Keystone State, is improving with wonderful rapidity. While Laramie county was yet a portion of Dacotah, Cheyenne, the "magic city," came into existence Minerva like and it is now town of large population and a, commercial mart for the Territory. Next in importance comes Laramie City, which is a growing place. Churches, schools manufactories and colleges flourish; the arts and sciences are propagated and newspapers flourish.

MINING AND STOCK RAISING

are subjects which engage much attention, and next year will be vast amounts of capital invested. The extensive deposits of coal, iron, copper and paint ore, only to be developed to expose riches will prove the assertion. Adjoining is the Eldorado of the new world.

RAWLINS SPRINGS

is the county seat of Carbon county — an enterprising little town of seven or eight hundred inhabitants. There are large buildings erected here for the use of the U. B. R. R. Co. and the works furnished employment to many men. We have a large hotel, college, school-house, a place of worship, a summer resort — at the springs, a public reading room, a literary society, and silver band that is second to none in the western country. This town is celebrated with being the only spot along the railroad, in Wyoming, where the noble red man ever came to grief. In different attacks on the town, the Indians were as many times repulsed with losses, and in no instance was a white man injured.

EVILNGSTON PHILLIPS,

whilom of the "oil regions," is one of our prominent citizens. He being an officer of railroad company, possesses superior facilities for obtaining knowledge as to the extent of our country's resources, and he pronounces the same to be rich. He and his accomplished lady are the life of our social circle and highly respected in community. Robert Baxter and many formerly of Titusville and other portions of Pennsylvania are also here. They are doing well.

RAILROAD LANDS.

To those persons who are desirous of seeking new homes — here in the Far West — will no doubt prove gratifying to learn that actual surveys of the lands as the Great Highway are soon to be made. These lands are alike suitable for grazing, agricultural purposes and mining. When in the market they will sell rapidly.

PAINT ORE.

A company from New York is taking large quantities of paint ore, which is designed for us in the manufacture of paint and Salamander chests. This article can be used for various other purposes.

THE WEATHER.

It is very cold here. The mercury at one time this month, stood at 28 degrees below zero. We are having the coldest weather known in this country for five years.   **C. E. W.**

The Titusville Herald, (Titusville, Pennsylvania) Feb. 18, 1871. —
Returned on a title wave it is time perhaps your correspondent be
again heard from. During the few weeks that elapsed since I had the
pleasure to communicate with your readers, there has marked change
in the business affairs of our young Territory. Now, instead of the in-
security to life and property, the social sluggishness that characterized
the frontiers in the early days, there appears to be vivacity, intelligence and refinement among the people, and business enterprise that
foretells prosperity. We have in the principal cities of the Territory,
manufactories, colleges, schools and fine art galleries, and the busy
hum of trade and commerce is heard everywhere.

In a few short years, it is confidently expected that the entrepot[4]
in Wyoming — Cheyenne — be connected with Helena, Montana, by
rail, and also connections with roads running east, as also means of
transportation for our mineral productions and yields from agriculture
pursuits and stock raising. A fine quality of wool will be gathered in
the present year. Sheep raising has been tried and proven a success.
To those who feel an inclination new life, new changes, and healthy

---

[4] a port, city, or other center to which goods are brought for import
and export, and for collection and distribution.

suits the fields of Wyoming presents rare inducements, as a perusal of Dr. Reeds report as Surveyor General will evince,[5] and to which attention is respectfully directed. Our climate is delightful, scenery beautiful (that no poet can deny) and nature, when in her more propitious mood presents varied charms to the painter, hunter, the mineralogist, the lover of piscatory and aquatic sports, and I am the philosopher who could find many pleasant walks without fear of stumbling over his patron rock.

With all these mirror-typed expositions however, the citizens, especially of Rawlins, are occasionally greeted with visits from our Indian "relations," and only weeks since a small band made a feint on the town, and indeed if the cold snap to the northward of us continues much longer we may expect many more of with their legendary tales and superstitious praying for an armistice, and proposing "terms" of peace, as they will need food. Those of your readers who understand Indian character, will doubtless conclude that the creatures have heard from Congress, but that's all a joke. There are lots of Red Cloud's "bummers" continually "around" picking up horses and occasionally a stray scalp. A funny incident occurred last Summer, and one which, singular as it was in its *denouement*, caused many old hunters to wonder on "the incertitude of human life." A colored girl whose name was Susannah was with a train of immigrants from Mobile *en route* for Oregon. While near this place they were attacked by Indians and

---

[5] reveal the presence of (a quality or feeling).

Susannah captured. An eye witness to the affair remarks afterwards that the girl was borne away triumphantly by a chief, in his arms. "When Sioux met Suse then came the hug of war. This is true.

It would surprise many to learn that we have away here in the Rocky Mountains some decided musical talent. On the night of the second, the Rawlins cornet band, assisted by amateur talent gave a grand concert in aid of Free Education. The selections were very fine, their rendition would defy criticism — almost. Especially the efforts, of Messrs. Devald, Elonington, Phillips, Esq., and other leading performers, were perfect and exquisitely and charmingly rendered. The vocal music was of no mean order. The affair, which was attended by persons from nearly every portion of the territory was a decided success, and will add largely to the effect desired, and to so noble a project as instructing the young.

From Utah the intelligence comes that fortunes are being made out of the silver mines near the city of Saints. Ever and anon the thud and heavy of burden trains is heard, the cars loaded with ore, seeking its way to the rapid strides that civilization has made the hitherto benighted regions of Mormonism (and which in due to the great measure providing for the constructing of Union Pacific Railway,) has given a fresh and sudden impetus to enterprise. Capital find sits way in there and receives its reward for hire. The streets of Salt Lake are alive with people, and the principal thoroughfare crowded with quartz brokers.

A due regard for the opinion of should impel writers to the observance propriety, so I must close my letter the promise of more anon.

                                                                              C. E. W.

Leavenworth Daily Commercial (Leavenworth, Kansas) 1 Sep 1871.

A PRACTICAL TEST.

The interesting letter from Wyoming Territory, of our correspondent now en route for California, contains a tribute to the practical workings of female suffrage in that Territory. The thing is working admirably. Those who were at first disposed to look with disfavor upon it are now becoming convinced in its favor from seeing its practical operation. As jurors, the women have given great satisfaction, both to the bench and the bar.

Lawrence Daily Journal (Lawrence, Kansas) 25 Apr 1871.

Missourians Killed and Captured by Indians.

From the St. Louis Republican, August 25.

A letter from Cheyenne, Wyoming Territory, informs us that the Indians are very troublesome in that vicinity; on the 27th of July, about fifty of them made an attack on eight white men, thirty miles south of Cheyenne, and killed three of them and captured three others. The remaining two made their escape. Among the killed was John Harris, formerly of St. Louis. The captured men were Peter Keller, from St. Joseph, Samuel Molt, from Newmarket, Mo., and a colored man, name not known. They have not been heard from since the affair.

Chicago Tribune (Chicago, Illinois) 27 Aug 1871.

A letter from Cheyenne, Wyoming, says : "One of our leading suffragists, the wife of a prominent citizen, and a most respectable and accomplished lady, created something of a sensation last week by promenading about town in company with the Mayor, the lady smoking meantime a fragrant Havana. It is understood that this eccentric feat was performed on a wager. There was nothing especially wrong about it, but some of the elders stood aghast with horror, and contemplative husbands were heard to murmur in pathetic tones, "What next?'"

The *Sun* (New York, New York) 30 Aug 1871.
Leavenworth Daily Commercial
(Leavenworth, Kansas) 8 Sep 1871.

The Great Creator never designed that one set of men should discover all the treasures of the earth, or that they should reap all the advantages which were designed for untold millions; for this reason, I always rejoice when I reflect that it is out of the power of any party of prospectors to discover all the treasures that are hidden in the earth's bosom.

-Letter from Wyoming Territory, 1872.

Women as Jurors.

In Wyoming Territory women can vote and serve as jurors.

How the thing works is pretty graphically described by a Cheyenne letter writer, and we invite attention to the following :

Harrisburg Telegraph (Harrisburg, Pennsylvania) 27 Jan 1872. — The Court convened on Monday morning, and the flutter caused by the sprinkling of ladies in the court room was apparent on the outside. Men were curiously standing at the doors and windows of the court - room to get a glimpse of the jurors in gowns. Mrs. A., Mrs. P., Mrs., H., Mrs. P., Mrs. W. and Mrs. C. were seated inside the bar; these only of the married ladies in town being at that time eligible to office.

As the clerk called the roll the ladies answered to their names and blushed. The docket was called and a murder case selected for trial. After a day spent in selecting, maneuvering, challenging and passing jurors for cause, a jury was finally completed, with three of these ladies in the list. Counsel were too gallant to challenge the ladies from a jury, and their gallantry has since become court etiquette in Wyoming.

Three days were occupied in taking testimony, and the evidence was nearly in when Mrs. H. was taken ill, and pronounced by her family physician too unwell to sit longer on the jury. Nature would assert itself, and Mrs. H. had to be excused and another juror drawn in her stead. The testimony was all retaken for the benefit of the new juror, and when completed a full week had been occupied in hearing this one case, at an expense to the county of over $1,000. As to the prisoner, serious fears were entertained that he would die on the jury's hands, rather than wait the verdict. It is still an open question whether these jurors are not liable to indictment for inflicting upon a fellow being "cruel and unusual punishment, contrary to the statute in such case made and provided." However, the prisoner survived a verdict of guilty in the first degree.

It was then for the first time discovered that one of these jurors was not a citizen of the United States. In their modesty, the counsel for the prosecution did not presume to ask such an important question. The only course now was for the court to order a new trial. But the prisoner voluntarily offered to plead guilty to murder in the second

degree, and accept a sentence of imprisonment for life, before endur-
ing another trial. This was accepted by the court, and Noyes went to
prison for life rather than be tried a second time by a female jury. As
to the husbands and children of these ambitious jurors, their case was
truly heart-rending, during the entire week they could neither speak
nor communicate with their loved and lost. At morning the door ways
of the court room was crowded with disconsolate husbands and children waiting to catch a glimpse of their wives and mothers as the
Sheriff brought the jury into court.

At night they would linger to gaze at the retiring forms that once
gladdened their homes and their hearts, as they were marched off by
the sheriff to the public hotel, to eat and spend the night together.
One husband became uncontrollable, and asked the judge to permit
his wife to go home and see her children and spend the night once
more but the judge was inexorable, and the poor husband returned
alone to his desolated fireside to indite a withering review of the
baneful results of Woman's Rights, which appeared in an evening paper on the following day. His argument was based upon the domestic
impracticability of the system, and upon the divine announcement that
it is not good for man to be alone.

During the entire week the ladies and gentlemen of the jury ate,
drank and slept under the guard of the Sheriff: the ladies all in one
room and the gentle men in another communicating. The day on
which the Court dismissed the jury was one of rejoicing on the part of

the afflicted. But home had lost its charms for their wives and mothers whose hearts had been turned by the flattery of counsel. And their heads filled with vain ambitions. The following week was spent by these exemplary women upon the streets and in public places, telling what happened in the jury, and what they knew about criminal law and the rules of evidence. They reminded one of a school boy with his first pair of red topped boots, or Young America with his first cigar."

Is not that a commentary on the "Woman's Rights" movement?

— From the Rutherford *Vindicator* we learn that on the 6th ult., a party of surveyors, near Fort Steele, in attempting to cross the Platte, while about the middle of the river, were carried below the ford by the deep and rapid current. Encumbered by books, instruments and heavy revolvers, only four of the party of seven succeeded in swimming to the shore. The others were drowned. One of the victims of this sad affair was Alfred F. Grayson, son of Rev. J. C. Grayson, of McDowell county, N. C. His body was recovered and buried at Fort Steele, Wyoming Territory. Mr. Grayson served with distinction in the Engineer corps of Lee's army.

The *Wilmington Morning Star*
(Wilmington, North Carolina) 19 Sep 1872.

Fossil Fishes.

A letter from Wyoming Territory, published in the New York Post, says: "Not far to the west of the Green River railroad station the rocks are filled with fossil fishes, in a wonderful-perfect state of preservation, so far as all their important characteristics are concerned. Of course they are flattened to the last degree, but their forms, including eyes, fins and scales, are perfectly preserved, so that the skillful naturalist readily refers them to their true place in the ichthyological scale. They occur in a finely laminated shale of a dingy yellow or drab color, and the dark-brown colored fishes show beautifully on this back-ground. One little slab now before me, only about four by eight or nine inches, shows parts of at least five of these beautiful fishes that have come down to us from a former age."

The *Indianapolis News* (Indianapolis, Indiana) 05 Nov 1872.

SECOND PAGE—Wyoming Letter: A November on the Mountains; Diamond Hunting; Mining Excitement—The Water Works [Communication]—Dr. Rauch and Our Sanitary Condition [Communication]—Boston: The Question of Relief; Chief Engineer's Report—The Storm at Duluth—Methodist Missions—The Horse Disease: Bonner and Bergh—General News Items.

Chicago Tribune (Chicago, Illinois) 19 Nov 1872.

WYOMING.

A November in the Mountains ---Diamond-Hunting--- Mining Excitement.

Finding Precious Stones --- Immense Tract to be Explored---Wild Animals.

Acquisitiveness of the Indians---Mormon Policy Toward the Redskins--- The Nauvoo Legion.

The Story of the Mormon Bible--Death of Washakie---His Character---Evanston and Its Surroundings.

From *Our Own Correspondent.*
EVANSTON, Wyoming Territory, Nov. 11, 1872.

Chicago Tribune (Chicago, Illinois) 19 Nov 1872. — A November in the Rocky Mountains may be in homely phrase as "snug." Wind from the snow-covered mountains howls dismally about, as if it were the abiding place of a million lost spirits wailing in agony. Snow glints and glistens, and creeps the crevices in the walls of the house, storm-clouds roll their appalling and gigantic forms across the face of Heaven. It is difficult to see anything at any considerable distance, on account of the falling snowflakes. The cottonwood and aspen trees have dropped their foliage, while the sturdy and upright pines seem to exult in their strength, and defy storms, coming from what direction they may as he who has a good covering over his head; thrice happy is the Shoshonee Indian skin-lodge is in perfect condition to bear up against the blast. Those lodges in the willow-thickets beside the icy streams look quaint enough, and the people therein appear contented.

Here I am going through the excitement of a fever, and my friends are hunting diamond mines. I have owned many silver mines and a gold mine in Wyoming Territory, and perchance I may get an interest in some. All of this sounds pretty but, when I state the fact that I never realize one dollar on all of my mining interests, certainly no one will envy me. I have paid out many a dollar to "honest miners" for working in my claims, and have done some pretty responsible work myself with pick and shovel, but yet to receive the first dime of income. Doubtless many people will ask, "Why do you delving when you have such poor success." The fact is, the sight of a string of mules laden with bacon, flour, sugar, and coffee, and a dozen bearded and resolute men, well and armed, and about to start for new is the very one thing on earth to the hair on an old miner's back. Do you think you could prevent his entering into the spirit of the thing? Oh, no, my friend! Human nature is very weak, and those miners would go to the "new diggings" if they knew it would "take the last button off of Gabe's coat." There is no resisting the impulse to pack up start off; and let me tell you, bear-hunting and deer-hunting, with all the excitement connected therewith, are nothing compared with and diamond-hunting. They do say that, the grand old range of the Uintah

Mountains, there are diamond-fields of immense extent and great richness. We shall see, and for I can say that we believe in them. It does good to become engaged in a real live mining excitement; there is nothing like it to make man stir around and bring the blood to the-surface; and nothing will be of much benefit to Wyoming Territory as these mines are supposed to be along the southern border. Should they prove to be rich, there will be an immigration hither next spring, and will be correspondingly brisk. To the miners, with their outfit, disappearing on road that leads over the hills, and thence round the base of the mountains, making trails and roads where there never was any before, rouses the old spirit of adventure in man's mind, and they carry with them our wishes for their success. They care for snow-storms or inclement weather, being bent on finding something which will enrich them and benefit their friends, and, at the time, add to the material wealth of the nation. They are true patriots.

Why should not there be diamonds in North America, as well as in Asia, Africa, and South America? I see no reason, and firmly be-lieve that they will be found, if they have not already been, in great numbers on this Continent. It said that the diamonds were first found in Africa by the children, who used them to play with, until, one day, a man came along who something about such matters, who that the little innocents were using fair-sized stones, of considerable value, their games. He wished to purchase the stones, but the parents of the children said they were of no value, and gave them to us at once. He gave the children some little presents, and went on his way a happier and richer man. Shortly afterward, the great furor about the South African mines broke out, and many diamonds of great value have been found therein. Some very handsome rubies have been found in Montana, and some diamonds of size in Idaho. It is also well-known that the soldiers of Cortez found some beautiful emeralds in the Mexican States of Chihuahua and Sinaloa. I see no such great obstacles in the way of finding fine gems in the heart of the Rocky Mountains, and believe, if they are not found now, they will be found hereafter by those who are earnest in their search.

The snow lies on the Uintah Range, and has filled up many of the gorges. As I write, I can see its magnificent outline resting against the sky, 40 or 60 miles away, and closing everything in on the south. Green River makes a great bend to the eastward, then runs southwest, and continues until it empties into the Grand River, or Rio Colorado, and thence on to the Gulf of California. This great stream runs through an immense extent of country which has never been explored. We are too apt to believe that we have made all the discoveries that can be made, but in this we are greatly mistaken; we know little or nothing about the resources of the southwestern portion of the National domain, and a land of great interest remains to be opened to civilization. There are several Indian tribes who have peculiar manners and customs, worthy of careful investigation and patient study, living, or roaming about, in this land; and there is more mineral wealth in it than has ever been dreamed of. The great bulk of the mineral wealth of the Nation will be found in and near the Wasatch range of mountains, and from the lateral ranges leading thereto, including the Uintahs. But this will require time. The Great Creator never designed that one set of men should discover all the treasures of the earth, or that they should reap all the advantages which were designed for untold millions; for this reason, I always rejoice when I reflect that it is out of the power of any party of prospectors to discover all the treasures that are hidden in the earth's bosom.

A young man who crossed the range a few days ago, reports that he was never out of the sound of the cries of the South American lions who were in the bushes near his trail, though he saw none of them. There appeared to be a great many of them, and their cries and growls were frightful. It is now too late for good fishing; the streams are covered with a coating of ice, and the trout are not considered good at this season of the year. They get, poor, and run down, and lose that delicious flavor which makes them so much better than any other fish that swims. In the depth of winter, however, they will sometimes take a fly which has been let down through a hole in the ice; but, as a rule, they are left undisturbed. The Indians scarcely ever interfere with them during the cold weather; but, when spring opens, they go after them with great good-will and zeal. I have seen a whole band on Snake River busily engaged fishing; and the salmon-trout taken in that stream form a considerable portion of the subsistence of the Snakes and Bannacks. These fish are but little different from the salmon taken in the lower portion of the Columbia River, though they are not so large, nor are they so carefully preserved, as the Indians about the Cascades make a regular business of catching, drying, and smoking them. They barter the dried salmon off for buffalo and deerskins which have been taken by tribes farther to the eastward, and do a good business. In old times, this was the greatest industry of the Indians, and they became expert traders as well as great cheats. Indians drive close bargains, and their generosity, so much talked about, is, so far as my experience goes, all a sham. An Indian never gives away anything without he expects four times as much in return. As a race, they are great beggars, receiving all things as a matter of course, but returning nothing. You may give a redskin ever so much, and the next day he will return for more. Their nature is a good deal like that of the horseleech, which is continually crying, "Give! give!" We all know with what nonchalance these knobby-nosed veterans receive everything that is presented to them on their visits to Washington, and with what peculiar grace they stow away their goods. There is no end to their capacity of reception, and anything from a needle to a finely-caparisoned pony is taken in without the slightest remorse of conscience. An Indian, richly dressed and riding on horseback, with a poor, broken-down squaw following him on foot, with a load on her back that would break down a mule, is not an inspiring spectacle, though it is by no means an uncommon one in the Rocky Mountains.

In a conversation which I had with a Mormon, a few days ago, he informed me that his people had adopted the policy, long since, of feeding, rather than fighting, the Indians. The Mormons have expended a vast amount of means and labor in locating farms, supplying

40

implements, and teaching them how to raise crops. This has been a great tax upon the whites. He said that almost every difficulty which had arisen between the Indians and the citizens of Utah had been the result of reckless and barbarous treatment by immigrants passing through the Territory, or by indiscreet and foolish persons residing therein. As early as 1840 and 1850 troubles broke out, and, after several persons had been killed, a peace was patched up by paying the Indians for the squaws who had been killed and the horses that had been taken off; and, by this means, further bloodshed was avoided. In 1853, another outbreak occurred among the savages, and several flourishing settlements were laid waste. In the settlements in the new valleys, the dignitaries of the Church have invariably advised the settlers to build forts, and locate themselves in sufficient numbers, and in such a way, that, when the Indians were on the war-path, they would be able to protect their families and their stock, besides being able to hold out until they could get assistance.

The savages were hostile again in 1865, and several settlers in Manti, Sanpete County. For a time, they were very troublesome indeed, and, though the Mormons did the best they could in their own defence, the Indians generally got the advantage. So well did they fight that the Mormons were driven north, and entirely abandoned their settlements in Piute and Sevier Counties. This occurred in 1807. It is pitiful to hear the Mormons tell of their wrongs, and I noticed this man never exulted over any of his foemen. Maybe this is true religion, but it requires a good deal of Christian charity to educate oneself up to the Mormons themselves believe that their religion is in some way connected with the Indians and that one of their missions on this earth is to civilize them and teach them the ways of peace. Notwithstanding all the harm they have received from the hands of the savages, they still seem willing to assist them, and appear more inclined than ever to welcome them as friends. They are sincere about this, as the Nauvoo Legion, composed for the most part of sturdy mountaineers, could, if they so willed sweep every Indian in Utah off the face of the earth within a twelvemonth. This Legion has one Lieutenant General, two Major Generals, nine Brigadier Generals, twenty-five Colonels, and one hundred and twelve Majors. It also has the proper number of company-officers. One-fifth of the Legion is cavalry, the rest infantry, with a few companies of artillery; and all of them are armed with the most approved modem weapons.

In a biographical sketch of President Joseph Smith, prepared by himself in 1812, in referring to the Mormon Bible, or Book of Mormon, he says: "In this important and interesting book, the history of ancient America is unfolded, from its first settlement by a colony that came from the Tower of Babel at the confusion of languages, to the beginning of the fifth century of the Christian era. We are informed by the records that America in ancient times had been inhabited by two distinct races of people. The first were called Jaredites, and came directly from the Tower of Babel. The second came directly from the City of about six hundred years before Christ. They were principally Israelites of the descendants of Joseph. The Jaredites were destroyed about the time that the Israelites came from Jerusalem, who succeeded them in the inheritance of the country. The principal nation of the second race fell in battle towards the close of the fourth century. The remnant are the Indians who now inhabit this country. But it will be seen that the Mormons, as a class, are inclined to look upon the Indian with a friendly eye; and, no very great while ago, they possessed great influence over them.

Washakie, Chief of the Shoshonees, or Snakes, is reported to have been killed on the reservation in the Sweetwater country a few days ago. He was a talented and brave man, and a sincere friend of the whites. His death is one of the greatest misfortunes which could have befallen his people. He was killed by an Indian who had refused to obey his order, and who had been guilty of some wrong, Washakie was quite an old man, and his whole efforts had been made for the advancement of the Indians. When a young man, he led several war parties, and gained a temporary ascendancy, and always afterward worked in such a way as to increase his authority. A rebellion broke out among the Snakes some time ago and a young man declared that he was a greater man than Washakie, and, further, that he was determined to be Chief of the tribe. He gathered about him several other young men, who all went off together, declaring that they would be no longer subject to the old Chief's authority. Washakie heard of it, and, mounting his horse, rode out at night and overtook the renegades, who were asleep. He immediately shot the leader dead, as he lay on the ground, and, as the others woke up, he called upon any one of them to dispute his authority. They were all thoroughly chapfallen, and followed the old man back to the reservation without further trouble. Perhaps his death was caused by one of the young men who followed off the new chief, whose attempted reign was so short and disastrous. On another occasion, Washakie saw a drunken Indian whipping his wife in the most cruel manner. He ordered the drunkard to desist, which he did for a short time, and then commenced whipping his wife again. Washakie again ordered him to stop, and this happened three or four times. At last the Chief got out of patience, and, noticing some movement on the part of the Indian which looked like an attack upon himself, he shot the Indian dead in his tracks. This action was looked upon with favor by all of his tribe.

I think Evanston is the most prosperous town in Wyoming Territory at the present time. New buildings are springing up in every direction, and the whole place has a business-like air about it. The coal-mines nearby have a great deal to do with the welfare of the town, and the hills near Bear River are filled with coal. The Union Pacific Railroad Company has some fine workshops here, and it is unquestionably the best place to have repairs made of any in the mountains. Moreover, it is quite a pretty town, and has what all travellers prize, — an excellent eating-house, where people who are travelling across the Continent can find something wherewith to refresh the inner man. The whole place bespeaks material prosperity; and the long view up Bear River, between the ranges of hills, is one of the finest on the whole railroad route. It is said that Evanston is the trading-point for between 7,000 and 8,000 people, consisting of railroad men, miners, lumbermen, and people living in the adjacent settlements. It is situated just at the eastern base of the Wasatch Range, and offers a fine field for stock-raisers. The soil is good, and the climate healthy. I cannot call it mild, as some of its friends do, though I am willing to say all I can in its favor. It is rapidly increasing in population, and there is some talk of building a large rolling-mill here. The Railroad Company has built a large hotel, and about twenty dwellings for its employes. The Evanston Lumbering Company is manufacturing a great amount of lumber, which it sells at reasonable rates. The logs are rafted down the stream to the mill from the great pine-forest a short distance above the town, on Bear River. It is really refreshing to be able to say something good of one of these frontier towns, and to be able to say that one of them is thriving and doing well. Such is the case with Evanston, which, three years ago, was as desolate a place as one could see.

Since writing the above, I have learned more about the diamond-fields. A party went out from Fort Bridger a few days ago, under the auspices of Colonel Brackett, Judge Carter and others, and the report came back that the diamonds have been found. I have just seen a letter from a gentleman who went to the mines who says: "The weather is so bad we cannot work the ground till spring. We picked up in three hours fifty carats of rubies, and twenty-six diamonds, one about three carats." The gentleman who wrote the letter is a diamond-dealer in New York. **ALGEBRA**

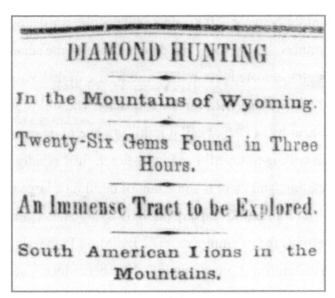

DIAMOND HUNTING

In the Mountains of Wyoming.

Twenty-Six Gems Found in Three Hours.

An Immense Tract to be Explored.

South American I ions in the Mountains.

The *Pittsburgh Daily Commercial* (Pittsburgh, Pennsylvania) 21 Nov 1872. — A letter from Evanston, Wyoming, of date November 11, contains some interesting facts and speculations concerning diamonds in the yet undeveloped regions of the Great West. The writer states that he has in his day been the owner of many so-called silver mines in Nevada, and a gold mine in Wyoming, but has never yet received a dollar of profit from any of them; yet, when he saw a string of males laden with bacon and flour, sugar and coffee, marshaled by a dozen bearded men, well mounted and armed, ready to start for the diamond alerts, he could not resist the temptation, and went with them, and. is now enjoying all the excitement of diamond hunting.

He says, "They do say that below the grand old range of the Uintah mountains there are diamond field of

IMMENSE EXTENT AND GREAT RICHNESS.

We shall see, and for myself I can say that I believe in them. Why should not there be diamonds In North America, as well as in Asia, Africa, and South America? I see no reason, and firmly believe that they will be found. If they have not already been, in great numbers on this continent. It is said that the first diamonds were found in South Africa by the children, who used them to play with until one day, a man came along who understood something about such matters, who found that the little innocents were using fair-sized stones, of considerable value, in their games. He wished to purchase the stones, but the parents of the children said they were of no value, and gave them to him at once. He gave the children some little presents, and went on his way a happier and richer man. Shortly afterward, the great furor about the South African mines broke out, and many diamonds of great value have been found therein.

RUBIES IN MONTANA — DIAMONDS IN IDAHO.

Some very handsome rubies have been found in Montana, and some diamonds of small size in Idaho. It is also well known that the soldiers of Cortez found some beautiful emeralds in the Mexican States of Chihuahua and Sinola. I see no such great obstacles in the way of finding fine gems in the heart of the Rocky Mountain, and believe, if they are not found now, they will be found hereafter by those who are earnest in their search.

The snow lies on the Uintah range, and has filled up many of the gorges. As I want, I can see its magnificent outline resting against the sky, forty or fifty miles away and closing everything in on the south. Green river makes a great bend to the eastward, then runs southwest, and so continues until it empties into the Grand river, or Rio Colorado, and thence on to the Gulf of California. This great stream runs through an immense extent of country which has never been explored. We are too apt to believe that we have made all the discoveries that can be made, but in this we are greatly mistaken; we know little or nothing about the resources of the southwestern portion of the national domain, and a land of great interest remains to be opened to civilization. There are several Indian tribes who have peculiar manners and customs, worthy of careful investigation and patient study, living, or roaming about, in this land; and there is more mineral wealth in it than has ever been dreamed of.

THE GREAT BULK OF THE MINERAL WEALTH

Of the Nation will be found in and near the Wasatch range of mountains, and in the lateral ranges leading thereto, in leading the Uintahs. But this will require time. The Great Creator never designed that one set of men should discover all the treasures of the earth, nor that they should reap all the advantages which were designed for untold millions; for this reason, I always rejoice when I reflect that it is out of the power of any party of prospectors to discover all the treasures that are hidden in the earth's bosom.

UNWELCOME SERENADES.

A young man who crossed the range a few days ago reports that he was never out of the sound of the cries of the South American lions who were in the bushes near his trail, though he saw none of them. There appeared to be a great many of them, and their cries and growls were frightful.

DIAMONDS AND RUBIES IN PLENTY.

Since writing the above, 1 have learned more about the diamond-fields. A party went out from Fort Bridger a few days ago, under the auspices of Colonel Brackett, Judge Carter, and others, and the reports come back that the diamonds have been found. I have just seen a letter from a gentleman who went to the mines, who says: The weather is so bad we cannot work the ground until spring. We picked up in three hours fifty carats of rubies, and twenty-six diamonds, one about three carats." The gentleman who wrote this letter is a diamond dealer in New York.

I do not remember a single instance where a jury of men has convicted either party for shooting at each other, even in a crowded room, if no one was killed; or for killing any one, if the victim had been armed. But with two or three women on the jury, they have never failed to follow the instruction of the Court. Again, the Courts have been nearly powerless, with only men for jurors, in enforcing the laws against drunkenness, gambling, houses of ill-fame, and debauchery in any of its forms. Neither grand nor petty juries could be relied on; but a few women on either panel changed the face of things at once; and from that day this kind of vice has trembled before the law and hidden itself from sight; while formerly it stalked abroad with shameless front and brazen confidence in protection from punishment.

-Letter from Wyoming Territory, 1873.

LETTER FROM WYOMING.

The Coal Fields of the West—A Stabbing Affair—Stock Raising—Wild Game.

Correspondence of the Union and American.

RAWLINGS, WYOMING, Jan. 24, 1873.—

Nashville Union & American. **(Nashville, Tennessee) February 4, 1873**. — It has been snowing for three days past, but is cold, and clear today. The trains are on time so far, but it is thought by many that they will be blocked before they reach here, as the snow is drifting very bad. The first quartz mill was put in operation in Seminole mines last week, and great excitement prevailed, but when they cleaned up all were satisfied with the result, and it only wants fine weather and a little capital to make this one of the best mining countries in the West. The superintendent said he could not tell exactly how much it would run to a ton of the best ore, as they had to crush a great deal of snow, ice and dirt. Coal has been discovered near the mines in a ravine. All that is required to get the coal is to drive a wagon up where it crops out and roll it in. This coal mine represents a long, wide ledge and has very little dirt on it, is of an excellent quality, and does not slack when exposed to the air. Near Seminole is one of the wonders of the great west. It consists of a large pine tree, petrified as it stands. It retains its natural color, but is soft and brittle as chalk. On the 20th inst., as No. 8 accommodation train was on its way from Green River to this place, a man came to the rear end of the train, came out of the car on the platform, drew a knife and tried to stab a brakeman named J. J. Duffy. As this man had the advantage, and the train was running twenty-five miles an hour, Duffy was in a delicate situation and had to jump off. The man then tried to kill Conductor Hall, but failed; then jumped off, but the brake beam hit him on the head and stunned him for a moment. The train stopped, and with the aid of the engineer and fireman he was bound and put in the car where the sheriff took charge of him. The engine was sent back for Duffy, and they found him safe and well.

THE GRAZING FIELDS OF WYOMING.

This Territory is unsurpassed for grazing purposes, cattle and horses turned out in the fall, after having been worked hard all summer, are driven up in the spring in fine condition. Beef cattle can be killed at any season of the year, being kept fat all the time, without a particle of hay. The grass in Bear river valley[6] is as high as the back of a horse. This grass cures on the stalk and forms an excellent hay on which the cattle feed during the winter. Grass does not take the second growth as in the States, but cures on the stalk in the field. It contains a great deal more nutriment than common hay, and cattle prefer it to any other kind of food. The game in this country is more abundant and fatter than in any other country. Trappers say the finest beaver and otter they can get they catch on Bear and Snake rivers. Numerous herds of horses and cattle exist in a wild state and are valuable as they are of fine breed and always in fine condition. A herd of 50,000 head were driven to this country from Texas, and grazed in this country during the summer. Several ranches have been put up and stocked with cattle, and are in a prosperous condition. After starting, it costs about $1.50 a head to raise these, and if driven to any

---

[6] They did not capitalize "river valley" in the name "Bear river valley."

railroad station, will bring from $15 to $25 per head. This is a better country than Texas, as very few cattle ever die. The climate is cool and pleasant throughout the summer. **J. E. D.**

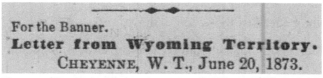

For the Banner.
Letter from Wyoming Territory.
CHEYENNE, W. T., June 20, 1873.

Jackson County Banner (Brownstown, Indiana) 02 Jul 1873. — WM. FRYSINGER, Esq. *Dear Sir*: Having an hour's leisure, I thought I would drop a line, in the hope that I may receive a long letter from you, giving me an account of the progress of the good people of Jackson county.

I receive the *"BANNER"* and the *"Democrat"* regularly. They are both good papers, and from them I gather much of the local affairs of my old home. I am glad to learn that Brownstown is improving. — Brownstown, for years past, has had a hard struggle. Her business men have been of comparatively small means, and the prejudice that has been attempted to be created against her has had its effect. But I hope her severe days are over, and that in the future her progress may be safe and sure, she has obtained wealth and prosperity sufficient to overcome all obstacles. Jackson county is one of the best counties in the State, and Jackson county people are as good people as there are any where. — If the spirit of jealousy, which I fear has grown to too great strength in some localities, could be put aside, and all the people look to the general prosperity and advancement of the whole county, instead of the advancement of some particular part of it, it would not be long until the whole county would be enjoying a greater state of thrift and enterprise than it ever has witnessed. When any public matter of improvement is to be considered, whether it be a Court House, a school house, a rail road, or anything else, it should be looked upon as being for the benefit of the whole county, and should receive the support of all the people of the county; and those who happen to be most favored by the location of it should not seek to use to the disadvantage of their friend and neighbors in other localities. The tendency of the spirit of jealousy and contention is to blast and destroy, and it should be given way to harmony and concord. If I know the desire of my own heart, it is that the highest state of happiness and prosperity shall be cast upon the people, who for twelve years extended to me help and kindness in a greater measure than I deserved.

I am very pleasantly situated, and I like this country exceedingly well. Cheyenne is situated on the Union Pacific Railroad, 516 miles from Omaha, 110 miles from Denver, and 1,260 miles distant from Sacramento. It is 6,041 feet above the level of the sea. The climate is delightful. There is none of the hot weather here that you have. This part of the Territory is one of the best grazing countries in the world. Horses, sheep and cattle grazing is carried on here extensively, and much money is made out of it. But the Territory is a mining, and not an agricultural country. — There is no timber in this part of the territory at all. But the mines are very rich. Gold and Silver are found, indeed, almost all the metals. Coal and cast iron exist here in inexhaustible quantities, and of the very best quality. The coal here is superior to the Pittsburg coal, and the iron ore is said to be of the very best quality. — It will not be many years until the mining interests of this Territory will be very great in deed. But I must close, or I will have written you a very long letter. I am going to Salt Lake City before long, and I will try and take items and send you an account of the country.

I was in Denver a few days since. It is a thriving place indeed.

I would be glad to have some of my friends make me a visit this summer. It would pay them to see this country.

Very truly,

JASON B. BROWN.

A letter from Wyoming Territory reports the appearance of a band of hostile Indians in the vicinity of Old Camp Brown on July 20th. They attacked a house and killed two women but retreated upon the approach of an armed body of men.

The *Daily Gazette* (Wilmington, Delaware) 4 Aug 1873.

Reports from Wyoming.

A letter from Colonel Brackett at Fort Stanleorgh, Wyoming territory, dated July 29, states that Colonel Wheeler and party returned from a scout in pursuit of the Indian murderers of Mrs. Richards and Miss Hall. He recommends a thorough scout of country to Fort Fetterman. General Sheridan, in forwarding the above, does not favor scouting, but recommends that the Indians about Forts Fetterman and Laramie be thoroughly whipped by our troops there. He says these Indians are the Sioux and their allies, the Arapahoes and Cheyennes, and he says there no Indians who deserve so richly a hard blow. General Sherman, in forwarding to the secretary of war, says he don't understand by what treaty or authority Indians are allowed to reside at Forts Laramie or Fetterman. They should be compelled to stay on a reservation.

Hartford Courant (Hartford, Connecticut) 13 Aug 1873.

Woman Suffrage.

HOW THE EXPERIMENT WORKS IN WYOMING.

The Pensylvania Woman Suffrage Association recently addressed Judo Kingham, of Wyoming, a letter asking his opinion of the working of the law admitting women to juries, and the following, which we take from the *Christian Union*, is his reply:

LARAMIE CITY,
Wyoming Territory, Dec. 26, 1872.

The *Washington Standard* (Olympia, Washington) 30 Aug 1873.

— Pennsylvania Woman Suffrage Association: It is now three years since the Act was passed giving women the right of suffrage, and the right to hold office in this Territory, in all respects the same as other electors. Under this law they have been elected, and appointed to various offices, and have acted as jurors and Justices of the Peace. They have very generally voted at all our elections, and have taken some part in the nominations; and although there are some among us who do not approve of it as a principle, I think there is no one who will deny that it has had a marked influence in elevating our elections, and making them quiet and orderly; and in enabling the Courts to punish classes of crime where conviction could not be obtained without their aid.

For instance: when the Territory was first organized, almost every one carried a loaded revolver on his person; and, as a matter of course, altercations generally resulted in using them. I do not remember a single instance where a jury of men has convicted either party for shooting at each other, even in a crowded room, if no one was killed; or for killing any one, if the victim had been armed. But with two or three women on the jury, they have never failed to follow the instruction of the Court. Again, the Courts have been nearly powerless, with only men for jurors, in enforcing the laws against drunkenness, gambling, houses of ill-fame, and debauchery in any of its forms. Neither grand nor petty juries could be relied on; but a few women on either panel changed the face of things at once; and from that day this kind of vice has trembled before the law and hidden itself from sight; while formerly it stalked abroad with shameless front and brazen confidence in protection from punishment.

There are, comparatively, so few women here, and those are so generally kept at home by domestic duties, that the Courts have been unable to obtain as many of them for jurors as was desirable. But those who have served have uniformly acquitted themselves with great credit. Not a single verdict, civil or criminal, has been set aside where women have composed a part of the jury. This has not been the case, by any means, when they have not been present. They have given better attention than the men have to the progress of the trials; have remembered the evidence better; have paid more heed to the charges of the Court; have been less influenced by business relations; and have exhibited a keener conscientiousness in the honest discharge of responsibility. And I have heard of no instance where they have incurred any odium, or ill-will, or want of respect, from having served as jurors. On the contrary, I am quite sure that they have been more highly respected, and more generally appreciated in consequence of it.

There is one other influence that has grown out of the presence of women in the Court room, both as jurors and as bailiff's, that has been most apparent and welcome; it is the quiet order and decorum, the decent and respectful behavior, the gentlemanly bearing that has always been observed in their presence. The spectators come there better dressed, chew less tobacco and spit less, sit more quietly in their seats, walk more carefully on the floor, talk and whisper less; and in all respects the Court room assumes a more dignified and businesslike air; and better progress is made in disposing of the matter in hand.

Certainly the whole effect on our courts and on our community, resulting from the participation of women in the administration of the laws has been most beneficial and satisfactory and it seems to me particularly proper that those who suffer most from the commission of crime and the evils of vice should take part in its suppression and punishment. There is another matter in which we have been greatly benefitted by this law, and that is the change it has wrought on election days, and its influence at the polls. Formerly our elections were scenes of drunken revel and noise; of fighting and riot. But when the woman came to vote, they were always treated with the attention and respect everywhere shown to women in the United States. If there was a crowd around the polls, they always gave way when a woman approached, and were silent and orderly while she deposited her vote and went away. If men became intoxicated, they did not remain there where the woman would see them. No noisy discussions would arise around the polls, because invariably, when a woman came up all such conversations would cease. The fact has been that very few people gathered at the polls; and noise and fighting, riot and drunkenness have been entirely unknown there. If men drank too much, as they sometimes did, they remained at the drinking-shops, each political party by itself, and consequently avoided the quarrels and collisions that so often occur, while the people went to the polls and voted as quietly as they go to church. This of itself has been a gain in our community of no small amount.

At first there was quite a number of women who refused to vote, but at every election that number has grown less, until now very few, if any, fail to exercise the privilege. Many refuse to vote as their husbands do, but I have not heard of any domestic discord or trouble growing out of such a course. In conclusion I wish to say, as broadly and as unqualifiedly as I can express it, that while I have seen a great many advantages and much public good grow out of this change in our laws, I have seen none of the evils or disadvantages so generally apprehended and so warmly denounced by the opponents of the measure.   **Very respectively,**

J. W. KINGMAN,
Asst. Justice U. S. Sup. Court Wg. T.

See First Page
  For interesting local items and Hon. J. B. Brown's letter from Wyoming Territory.

Jackson County Banner (Brownstown, Indiana) 5 Nov 1873.

Jackson County Banner **(Brownstown, Indiana) 5 Nov 1873.** —
WM. FRYSINGER — My Dear Sir: I have collected together some
information in regard to the material resources of this Territory,
which, if you think of sufficient importance. I would be glad to present to the people of Jackson county, by means of the BANNER, that
welcome visitor to Jackson county people.

BOUNDARIES, AREA AND
SURFACE ASPECT OF WYOMING.

Wyoming reaches into the Rocky Mountains, westward to the
eastern rim of the Salt Lake Basin, nearly four hundred miles, or
seven degrees of longitude, with Nebraska and Dakota on the east,
and Utah and Idaho on the west. North and south she spreads over
four degrees of latitude with Montana on the north, and Colorado and
a part of Utah on the south.

Her area covers 97,882 square miles, being as large as Ohio, Indiana. Massachusetts. Connecticut, and Rhode Island combined.

Within the mountains of Wyoming are situated three great table
land plains or basins, the Laramie Plains, and Platte River Valley, extending from near Sherman along the railroad to Creston, as large as

Massachusetts; the Green River Valley, extending west from Creston to Piedmont, and from the Colorado line north to the head of Green and Sweetwater Rivers, with an area of about nineteen thousand square miles, and largely underlaid with lignite coal; and the Big Horn Valley, larger than the State of Connecticut, partly underlaid with coal, and fertile as the Great Salt Lake valley. The Big Horn Valley is surrounded by the Big Horn Mountains. The entire Big Horn Country is now in the possession of the Indians. But little mining prospecting has been done in these mountains, the miners having been, in every instance, driven out or massacred by the Indians. But it has been ascertained from information entirely reliable that the Big Horn Mountains abound in gold, in quantity and quality, equal to the California or Montana mines. Silver and copper have been found in great quantities in these mountains, and I have no doubt but that as soon as a treaty can be effected with the Indians, by which the Big Horn Country can be opened up, that there will be developed in these mountains some of the richest gold, silver and copper mines that can be found anywhere in the United States.

No rivers of importance rise in Wyoming except in the northwest corner, in the Wind River Mountains, near Fremont's peak. Here the Yellowstone, Green and Sweet water Rivers, and some branches of Snake River, take their rise.

Green River Basin is the drained bottom of a vast fresh water, lake within the mountain regions during the tertiary period, at which time the extensive lignite coal deposits known to exist there were formed. This great basin became dry land by some fracture in the Minta range of mountains south of Wyoming, through which the waters found their exit, and cut out the Green River canons. Nearly the whole of this basin is covered with sage, with grass only along the streams.

AGRICULTURE AND STOCK RAISING.

That portion of Wyoming between Nebraska and the mountains is as well adapted to purposes of agriculture as Colorado. The country slopes northward from Cheyenne, to the Yellowstone River, and all the valleys of the numerous streams which enter this region from the mountains are suited to the production of small grains, and well adapted to the raising of all kinds of vegetables. Vegetables grow to an enormous size. From two to four hundred bushels per acre of the best quality of potatoes can be raised and turnips, parsnips, and all other garden vegetables do equally well, the soil is remarkably well adapted to the large yield of wheat, barley and oats, because of its favorable combination of materials which make up a good argillaceous and calcareous soil with the addition of potash and gypsum, which are derived from the decaying calciferous and feldspathic rocks of the mountains, the seasons are short, and generally it is necessary to resort to irrigation. This is easily accomplished in the valleys of all the streams, by taking the water into sluices and spreading it out wherever necessary, as is so successfully done by the Mormons in the Salt Lake Valleys. The table lands, though better situated for grazing purposes will to some extent be irrigated and brought under cultivation in coming years, by means of artesian wells, now practiced quite extensively in many parts of California. But, if the ground is plowed deep and subsoiled, in many seasons irrigation will not become necessary in many of the low valleys, the Valley of Crow Creek will raise fine potatoes without irrigation; and back of the City of Cheyenne, on still higher ground, better potatoes have been raised without irrigation than are usually raised in many of the Western States.

MOUNTAIN RANGES.

the mountains of Wyoming have not the average altitude, nor are they so compactly clustered together, as those of Colorado. The highest are Fremont's Peak, in the Wind River Range, 13,000 feet in altitude, Laramie Peak and Elk Mountain, 11,000 feet, and the central portions of the Medicine Bow and Big Horn, 12,000 feet.

THE LARAMIE RANGE,

on which Sherman is located, is a continuation of the Colorado Snowy Range, west of, and around Long's Peak. Its course is nearly north and south. Its general width is nearly eighteen miles, until it reaches Laramie Peak, where it spreads out, a portion tending to the northwest, toward Fort Fetterman and the Big Horn Range, and a portion tending west to meet Seminoe Mountains at the canon of the North Platte. Its height varies from 7,000 to 9,000 feet.

THE MEDICINE BOW RANGE

is also a northern extension of the Colorado Mountains, and Elk Mountain is its northern extremity. Its course is north and south; its length, fifty miles, and width about twenty-five miles. Its snow clad summit is always visible from Sherman and Laramie City, in a western direction. It lies east of the North Platte, and west of Laramie River, and in range with the eastern mountain rim of the North Park of Colorado. Its summits range from 8.000 to 12,000 feet in altitude. The Medicine Bow like the Minta Range, is heavily timbered, though most of the timber is more suitable for railroad ties and telegraph poles than for sawing purposes.

[TO BE CONCLUDED NEXT WEEK.]

WYOMING TERRITORY:
Her Material Resources.

CONCLUDED.

CHEYENNE, W. T., }
October 8, 1873. }

Jackson County Banner (Brownstown, Indiana) 12 Nov 1873. — The cluster of mountains forming part of the continental divide, between Bridger's Pass, south of Rawling's Spring Station and the North Park of Colorado, have no well defined name. Some have called them the "Mintas" of Wyoming; others have termed them the Grand Encampment Mountains, because the timber men of the Union

Pacific Railroad obtained, years ago, bridge timber and ties on Grand Encampment Creek, which heads in these mountains, west of the North Platte, and gave the name of Grand Encampment to them, but they form a portion of the crest of the continental divide, and are therefore really part and parcel of the Sierra Madre of the Rocky Mountains. In looking southwest from the crest of Elk Mountain, you have a fine view of this portion of the Sierra Madre, with snow capped peaks the year around, and spreading out over thirty miles in width, east and west, along the southern boundary of Wyoming. They form a part of the northern and western rim of the North Park of Colorado, and continue southward on the west side of the North Park, forming a continuous, but circuitous rim between the North, Middle, and South Parks, and continue on, as the water-shed of the Rocky Mountains, through New Mexico.

THE SEMINOE MOUNTAINS

derive their name from one of Freemont's old guides of that name, who led him out of Sweetwater Valley, through Seminoe Pass, (now frequently called "Whisky Gap,") and thence southeastward to the Parks of Colorado. These mountains lie between Seminoe Pass and Platte River, twenty miles in length, and fifteen miles south of Sweetwater River, at Independence Rock. They tend westerly, and the range continues nearly to the head of Sweetwater, at South Pass, and takes the name of the river west from Seminoe Pass. The highest peaks in the range are 10,500 feet in altitude; Bradley's Peak, 9,500 feet, and Young's Peak over 9,000 feet.

THE BIG HORN MOUNTAINS.

are the largest, longest and most conspicuous mountains of Wyoming. Their shape much resembles that of a horse shoe, the open space on the west being closed by the Snowy Range, which runs-northward from the Wind River Chain, and divides the Yellowstone Park Basin from that of the Big Horn Basin on the east. They almost encircle the Big Horn Basin, the south rim being severed by the canon of Wind River, the northern one by the Big Horn River canon, over thirty miles in length, which commences near the northern boundary of Wyoming, and passes into Montana. They are the production and mere extension of the same upheaval forces that sent up the Laramie and Medicine Bow Ranges on the south, partially dying out north of the Red Buttes, yet clearly showing an anticlinal axis from the latter point, northwest to the nearest point of the Big Horn Range. Here the internal forces appear to have divided, one branch trending on its northwesterly course to the Big Horn canon, the other striking on westerly to join the Wind River Range at the head of Wind River. In these mountains are destined to become an immense store-house of wealth to the people of Wyoming, when the wild and warlike Sioux Indians shall cease to occupy them as hunting grounds.

THE WIND RIVER RANGE.

This range forms the continental water shed or divide between Idaho and Montana, and trends southeast into the northwest part of Wyoming, terminating at the old South Pass and the head of the

Sweetwater. The same line of upheaving force continues southeasterly from the railroad at Creston and Separation, as is seen in the direction of Bridger Pass and the North Park of Colorado. Freemont's Peak, in latitude 43 30 north, longitude 110 west from Greenwich, is 13,000 feet in altitude, and much of the highest part of this range, constituting, in fact, the initial point of three grand watersheds, from, which flow branches of the Columbia, the Colorado, and the Yellowstone Rivers. Green River heads near this Peak, and drains an area of over fifteen thousand square miles, while the affluents of the Yellowstone drain an area of over twenty thousand square miles in Wyoming.

THE SNOWY RANGE.

This forms the eastern rim of the Yellowstone Park, and divides it from the Big Horn Valley on the east. It is an arm of the Wind River Chain, trending off northwardly toward the Yellowstone River below the falls, and part of which turns to the northeast to join the Big Horn Mountain.

THE MINTA MOUNTAINS.

This range lies along the southern boundary of Wyoming, extending from Green River west to the Wasatch Mountains, over a hundred miles. Its trend is almost due east and west, and its general course straight. The main portion of the mountain is within Minta, though, for practical purposes, it is a Wyoming Mountain. Its northern face or slope is approachable only from Wyoming, and this part is heavily timbered. Four considerable streams rise in the axis of this mountain, and run down its northern slope into Wyoming, to wit: the Bear River of Salt Lake, and Black's, Smith's, and Henry's Forks of Green River. The latter stream rises by three forks, the east one having its source at the base of Gilbert Peak. The valley of this branch encloses one of the most beautiful of a series of mountain lakes which exist in this vicinity, this one having an altitude of 11,000 feet. The crest of this mountain furnishes several snow clad peaks of great beauty, the white domes of which can be seen through all the summer months from the railroad, though sixty miles distant. Gilbert's Peak, at the head of Henry's Fork, rises 13,182 feet; Cox's Peak, farther west, rising like an immense dome, is 13,250 feet; and Dawes' Peak, still farther west, rises 13,300 feet. Yet farther west is Logan's Peak, at the head of Bear River, rising 13,500 feet. The limit of arborescent. vegetation on most of these interior mountains is 11,000 feet. Thus the snows on the north side lie upon 2,500 feet in height on bare surface, and not hidden from view by the dense forests which often cover the mountain up to the arborescent line.

Near Logan's Peak are open spaces where one can obtain some of the grandest views on the continent. Looking west you have the Valley of Bear River at your feet, while over the summits of lower ranges the Wasatch Mountains, east of Salt Lake City, and along the high crest between Parley's Park and the Cottonwood Canons, can be clearly seen fifty miles distant; also, the snowcapped summits at the head of the American Fork, Proo Canon, and the several snow peaks along the range as far south as Mount Nebo, Utah, which is so prominent in the distance southeast of Utah Lake. Looking north with a field glass, you behold in the far distance the snow clad mountains of the Wind River Range, extending along the horizon in the vicinity of Freemont's Peak, at least one hundred and eighty miles away. To the northeast you have spread out before you the plains of Green River Basin, to the continental divide at Creston, over two hundred miles ; and on the east loom up the snow clad peaks west and north of the North Park of Colorado, not less than one hundred and seventy-five miles distant. No one, except the beholder, who is familiar with the topography of these distant points, and is well assured that no prominent object intervenes between him and the grand one in view, can possibly appreciate the astonishing extent of country over which the eye, by the aid of a good field glass, can travel through the pure, clear atmosphere of these high altitudes. All of the mountains of Wyoming abound in gold, silver and copper, as well as many other valuable minerals; and it is believed by the best mining explorers and prospectors that the best and most valuable mines of Wyoming are yet undiscovered.

TIMBER AND WATER RESOURCES.

A stranger passing over the Union Pacific Railroad through this territory for five hundred miles, would naturally infer that it contained no timber, for there is scarcely any to be seen from the road. It exists, however, in great abundance from twenty-five to one hundred miles from the railroad, and can be brought to the road very readily from the heads of the streams which cross it. The Big Laramie and its branches head in great forests of timber, if the Medicine Bow and Colorado Mountains, and probably a million of ties per annum are floated down to the railroad at Laramie City, and the village of Wyoming. The mountains north and west of Laramie Peak contain large quantities of fine timber, of larger size than that of the Medicine Bow Range, the mountains which flank the North Platte, all the way to the head in North Park, are largely covered with timber. The head branches of Green River rise in the southwest face of the Wind River Mountains, in the midst of extensive, and valuable forests. The Big Horn Mountains are well supplied with forests of timber. The timber in all the mountains differs very little in variety, consisting principally of pine, cedar, fir, and hemlock.

The Territory possesses a large amount of water, but very few water power mills. There is plenty of water power near the sources and at the lower canons of the North Platte and the two Laramie Rivers, Green and Bear Rivers that afford a considerable water power near their sources, and Wind, Big Horn, Tongue, Powder, and Cheyenne Rivers present a reasonable amount. All these water power privileges will be appropriated as the country settles up, and side railroads penetrate to their vicinity.

But I must close. I would like to write about many other things of interest to this Territory, but I have already extended this letter to such length that it will crowd out much matter of more interest to your readers than it is. For the information contained in this letter, I am

mainly indebted to Mr. Silas Reed, the Surveyor General of this Territory. Dr. Reed has been Surveyor General of Missouri and Illinois.
He is one of the old time gentlemen, accomplished and obliging, full
of information and learning, and ever ready to encourage and assist. I
find in him a most valuable companion.

JASON B. BROWN.

*I scarce know how to describe this most beautiful and enchant-
ing place.*

-Letter from Wyoming, 1874.

The Great Geysers in Eruption.

One of the most interesting exhibi-
tions of the Yellowstone region will be
given at Laing's Hall this evening.
Among the views to be exhibited are the
hot springs, Yellowstone canyon, boiling mud lakes, the great falls of the
Yellowstone, Hayden's exploring party
standing before Old Faithful in eruption, magnificent mountain scenery,
views of the Park, besides a large number of others equally as interesting.
Mr. J. Savage, who was one of the party,
will be present to explain the views.
Admission will be 25 cents. Children
10 cents. Tickets for sale at Crew &
Morgan's, and Brown's drug store.

Leavenworth Daily Commercial (Leavenworth, Kansas) 6 Mar 1874.

A letter from Cheyenne, written by Daniel McLaughlin, to Major Bruce, appears in the Bozeman *Avant Courier*, upon the subject of Big Horn and Yellowstone exploration, in regard to which the Cheyenne and Wyoming people were all alive and anxious. Efforts were being made to obtain permission from the Secretary of the Interior for an expedition from Cheyenne to cross the country, via Forts Fetterman, Phil. Kearney, and C. F. Smith, to the objective point on the Yellowstone river, and to unite with the Montana Expedition in making an established route for trade and travel between Cheyenne and Bozeman. It was confidently expected that several expeditions, having those objects in view, would shortly leave Cheyenne, as connection between those two cities was greatly desired.

Congress has established a mail route between Cheyenne and Boreman, via Fort Fetterman, and it was expected that service would be ordered on the route the coming spring or summer.

Deseret News (Salt Lake City, Utah) 11 Mar 1874.

A Singular Case of Disappearance.

Los Angeles Herald (Los Angeles, California) 19 Mar 1874. —
Napa Register of the 12th says: A most singular case has just tran-
spired, involving the sudden disappearance of an old and well-known
citizen of Napa. J. F. McCort, merchant tailor, opposite the *Register*
office, on Main street, left here a week ago last Monday morning, as
he said, for San Francisco, to buy goods. He was looked for all last
week, but did not return as was expected, and nothing was known of
his whereabouts until last evening, when Postmaster Brown received
a letter from Laramie, Wyoming Territory, which throws light upon
the situation. The letter is dated March 7th (last Saturday), and states
that a man had been left there that morning by the eastern-bound train
who was evidently very insane. The railroad authorities took him
from the train and turned him over to the City Marshal. He was ex-
amined by a doctor, gave his name as John F. McCort, a business
man, and tailor by trade, and referred for his standing in town, to
Brown, Postmaster. He had money, appeared like a man of intelligence, and wore the badge of a Royal Arch Mason. He had been hurt
on the shoulder, and said he had been thrown from a buggy. Brown's
informant, however, adds later that he had learned from the conductor
that McCort jumped from the train the night before, while they were
running, and the fall injured his side and shoulder. They backed up
and got him on the train again, and brought him on to Laramie.

Independent-Journal (Ottawa, Kansas) 13 Aug 1874. — Editor Ottawa Journal: On the morning of the 24th, a jolly crowd of us young folks, numbering thirty, left the city of Virginia Dale, some thirty miles southwest of here, on a general fun expedition.

The party consisted of about an equal number of ladies and gentlemen. The railroad not having penetrated that portion of the Rockies, we went in buggies, spring wagons and carriages, each wagon containing three couples. For the first twelve miles our road lay along the

UNION PACIFIC RAILROAD,

through the beautiful valley of the Laramie; then verging a little, west, we struck the old Salt Lake trail. After travelling this some two miles, we came to Lake Station, or what was once a station in the palmy days of the rollicking stage coach. It took its name from a beautiful lake on the west side of the road. At present there are no buildings, except a small house on the bank of the lake, and between it and the road. On the opposite side of the road the station proper stood. The skeleton of the stables still stands, a monument of departed greatness, while the site of the station is still plain to be seen, and from the size of which one is led to believe it to have been one of considerable proportions. Could these ruins, and the little house on the lake shore talk, no doubt they could "a tale unfold" which would be interesting, if not tragical. One important feature which made this place a good stopping point for stages, is a

CLEAR CRYSTAL SPRING

which bubbles up on the bank of the lake, furnishing plenty of that indispensable luxury for both man and beast, cold water. After regailiug ourselves at this fountain, we again went whirling over hill and through dale, fun and mirth being the ruling element in that crowd of fun-seeking lads and lasses.

About twenty miles from here, we struck the "summit," and just here we were struck by a slight rain storm, which, however was of short duration, and, thanks to our umbrellas, we passed through without damage to our linen. On this summit one of the most beautiful panoramic views I had yet seen in the far famed Rockies, burst upon our view. Away to the west it stretched out with its hills and hollows, its trees and rocks, dales, canons, and beautiful plains covered with luxuriant grass, where now the deer, the elk, the antelope, the puma, or rocky mountain lion, and black and cinnamon bear roam, and where the hunter with his trusty rifle is won't to hie[7] for this noble game. From the summit we gradually descended, sometimes in a

---

[7] Go quickly.

deep gorge, with high and almost perpendicular walls of rock on either side, shutting off our view from all but the vaulted heaven above,
and the narrow, crooked road before and behind us, until finally we
find ourselves in a beautiful dell, or valley, with a murmuring little
brooklet speeding its way between grassy banks to the mighty ocean.
After traversing this dell for a mile or more, we suddenly find ourselves confronted with the end, as it were, and are forced to climb a
steep hill finding ourselves on an elevated plateau of perhaps ten
miles in extent; then we descend once more into another beautiful little valley, and thus we go on until between two and three o'clock p.
m., we entered

VIRGINIA DALE.

I scarce know how to describe this most beautiful and enchanting
place. It was once a stage station on the Omaha and Salt Lake road.
It is simply a vast basin with huge mountains looming up on two
sides. A little stream, called Dale Creek, runs across it, and along the
banks of this stream lies the road, the only passable inlet or outlet to
it. It is occupied at present by a Mr. Leach, who has a dairy. The
place has its history, and if true, a sad one to some. On the eastern
side a high rock, called

LOVERS LEAP

so named from the fact that a couple of lovers, not being able — in
consequence of a little "unpleasantness" on the part of "pa" and "ma"
to journey through life together, concluded to take that journey from

whence no traveler returns. These lovers — tradition tells us — belonged to an emigrant train en route, to the golden West, and at this point forbearance ceased to be a virtue, and they concluded to take their destiny in their own hand, and, climbing to the top of this rock, with arms lovingly entwined around each other, made that awful leap of 600 feet down, down, down, to eternity. I stood where they stood and looked down that awful abyss and shuddered to think that from this point

> *"Two souls with but a single thought, Two hearts that beat as one,"*

had taken their flight to the world beyond, and thus ended a life which had become a burden.

A splendid view is had from the top of this rock, stretching from the north in a semi-circle to the south. Immediately to the west are two large mountains, seemingly of solid rock and of a square shape, like some huge barn minus the roof. Then there are valleys, trees, hills, etc., like some billowy sea convulsed by a tornado. At this place we passed our first night. We had one tent which accommodated some of the ladies, while others passed the night in the house of Mr. Leach. Everything passed off lovely, and at a little after six o'clock the next morning we were on our way to

THE FISHING GROUNDS,

which we reached at about 11 o'clock a. m., without serious accident, more than the giving out of one of our horses, which we exchanged for another, and all went well. Before dinner some of the boys and ladies were off with the hook and line tempting the speckled trout, and were successful in catching some of the beauties, which were served up in a palatable style by the ladies, and we had a sumptuous repast. During the afternoon about one-half of the crowd started on the return trip and arrived home about 9 p. m., while the balance of us remained, fished, rambled over the rugged mountains, or lounged about camp, as best suited the inclinations of each. Our camp was pitched in a beautiful valley called

"BUFFALO MEADOW."

Here we passed the second night. The party were successful in enticing nearly two hundred of the delicious trout from their watery homes, and we fared sumptuously. Anyone who has not had the pleasure of eating brook trout cannot imagine how delicious they are, whilst to those who have feasted on them it would only be an aggravation to speak of them. On the morning of the third day, we struck our tent, loaded up the traps, fish, and lastly, ourselves, and started on our homeward journey. About two miles from our camp we saw the first game worth shooting, an antelope, and one of the boys soon made for him, but failed to bring him down. About 11 a. m, we arrived at Sherman, a station on the U. P. Railroad, where we stopped and took dinner at the

SHERMAN HOUSE.

Mine host, Mr. Nash, getting us up a capital meal to which we did ample justice. This is the highest railroad point on the U. P., and I believe the highest in the world, being 8,235 feet above the sea level.

After dinner we started for Laramie, intending to stop on the way in some of the many beautiful valleys and spend a few hours in pleasantry as inclination might prompt, but in this we were doomed to disappointment. After leaving Sherman some three miles, the foremost wagon — or the boys in it — espied some deer off to the right, and immediately started for the game, two wagons following over the gently undulating prairie; but, after waiting some time for their return, one wagon started on, the other waiting. A mile or two on, a heavy rain came up, which put all thought of a pleasant time in some green and flowery dell out of our minds; so, hoisting our umbrellas and wrapping our blankets about us, prepared to accept what might come, and, as the old saying is, "it never rains but it pours," it did in this case. For a few minutes it seemed that the heavens literally let loose with the intention of giving us a good bath, but thanks to our protection, we came out all right. Not so with the hunters, for they were unprotected even by a coat, and received the contents of the cloud as it came. After the shower they built a fire and soon dried their garments. Without further mishap we all arrived home, and voted it, as a picnic, a grand success, so far, at least, as fun and enjoyment are concerned, and all are anxious for another, which is already being talked up, the objective point being "Sheep Mountain," some thirty miles west of here. And thus began and ended my first picnic to the grand old Rockies.

The spring and summer have been quite dry here until the past three or four weeks, which have been exceeding rainy. Vegetables are looking fine and the farmers are in good spirits over the prospect for a fair hay crop and plenty of feed for stock during the winter. Business here is good. There is a fair prospect now of the U. P. Railroad company erecting rolling mills at this point, which will add another item of interest to the city of Laramie.

Respectfully,

DILL H. JAMES.

The *Burlington Free Press* **(Burlington, Vermont) 25 Sep 1874 —** RAILROAD TRAMPS. There is not a railroad in the United States that suffers more from professional dead beats and " tramps," as they are called here, than the Union Pacific. Friendless, moneyless, bereft of all ambition, haggard and worn, with clothes of which the original color must remain a matter of conjecture, they troop along in couples and triplets, and often only a single figure is outlined against the horizon. Where they come from or where they are journeying is a matter of still greater mystery, as some of them are often seen passing section-house for food and sleep well, they and repassing. They besiege every station and sleep almost any place when night overtakes them.

They are constantly upon the watch for opportunities to steal a ride upon the trains, and but for the vigilance of the train men they would soon arrive at their destination or the end of the line. Some of them manage to ride, and the means they employ are often as dangerous as novel. They will climb up the roof of a car after night and hang on the stove-pipe or anything that is available, and ride until detected. The eastward bound passenger train stopped here one morning for water, when one of the brakemen walking along the train discovered a man snugly ensconced in the locker under the baggage car. He was wakened from a sound sleep and informed that he had reached his destination. He deliberately crawled out, shook the dust from his hair and clothes, and took a look at the surrounding country. Just then the train started up, and he, concluding to go on, crawled back into the locker while the train was in motion, but the sharp eye of the brakeman brought him to grief. The train was stopped and he was once more invited to remain in this city. Upon interviewing him I learned that he had ridden in the locker from Green River, over 200 miles. He turned his pockets for evidence of cash, but a solitary nickel only made its appearance. He begged for a crust of bread, only a crust, and got it. He lingered about until a passing tram going his way came along, when he disappeared somewhere in the joints of its long, huge back, and was gone. They have all kinds of stories to tell that would wring pity from the heart of any one, if they did not have the professional ring. Some of them are really the victims of misfortune, and deserve assistance, but this is a poor country for a pitiful mouth, and sympathy is a stranger in the land. Hard work, much profanity, old clothes, and whiskey abound upon the line of the Union Pacific road through the mountains. Yet there are redeeming features. Good officers, gentlemanly and large hearted train men are the rule and not the exception. I think I am safe in saying that the Union Pacific road can compare with any road in this respect. — *Wyoming letter.*

THE BLACK HILLS.

RENEWED RUMORS OF GOLD.

NEW YORK, Oct. 8.

A letter from Cheyenne, Wyoming Territory, states that it is the general belief there that there is gold in the Black Hills, and companies of two hundred and three hundred are forming in that Territory and Dakota to go there and to Big Horn mountains. The preference being given to the latter.

Buffalo Evening Post (Buffalo, New York) 8 Oct 1874.
Boston Post (Boston, Massachusetts) 9 Oct 1874.
Newport Daily News (Newport, Rhode Island) 10 Oct 1874.

FROM WYOMING TERRITORY.

The Black Hills Country, and Gen. Custar's Expedition—A Glittering Fraud—Mineral Richness of Wyoming—Some Advice.

ROCK SPRINGS, WYOMING TER.,
November 18, 1874.

Concordia Empire **(Concordia, Kansas) 27 Nov 1874.** — EDITOR EMPIRE — DEAR SIR: As promised to let you know something about the Black Hills country when I should arrive in Wyoming Territory, I will, from time to time, send you all the news I can hear on the subject, as I shall winter in a mining camp at this place, where I can "post" myself and you.

You ought to be here and hear the loud "haw! haw!" from veteran prospecters and old miners and frontiersmen, when they see men from the East and read the charming descriptions of Gen. Custar's march through the Black Hills. The correspondents who sent those glowing descriptions to the Eastern press possibly imagined that it was a new and unknown country of which they were writing; but I have seen a hundred men in Wyoming Territory who have been through it in different directions. In 1865 Gen. O'Connor made a thorough reconnaissance of much of that region in his Tongue River expedition. Many of his men are here in Wyoming Territory today, and they say that there is no gold there; to which general statement I add the direct testimony of a score of good men, in whom I have confidence, that

85

the country contains no fertile land worth speaking of; so you can see what they think of Gen. Custer's reports here I think, however, that Wyoming Territory is very rich in gold and silver, copper, plumbago, iron and coal. I am sinking a shaft for the U. P. R. R. Co. at Rock Springs, and at the depth of 35 feet I have gone through four veins of good coal, one three feet, one two feet, one four feet and one seven feet, in thickness in all sixteen feet of good coal. Also, I have seen gold, silver and copper ore that came from the Sweetwater, Bear, Wind and Snake rivers, some of which will pay $5,000 to the ton. It is said, too, that there is good farming land. In the valleys, that it is a good stock country, and that game and fish are plenty. I mean to visit that region soon. There are some suspicious circumstances connected with the Black Hills reports. Sioux City and Yankton have had gold discovered there every summer for the past five or six years, giving occasional hints as to the advantages of those places for "outfitting." When I was at Cheyenne City, just after Gen. Custar's discoveries, the friends of that metropolis demon-stinted by the maps that it was by all odds the nearest place to the richest diggings, and that it had the best natural roads to the gold fields so I think it well to consider these points. Well, if there are any young men in Kansas that are selling out to start to the Black Hills, I would suggest that they stop until next Spring at least. If there is any gold there it won't all be taken away before that time. The first comers will have a job on hand with the Indians to last them the first six months.

Yours truly,   **J. K. Watson.**

Leavenworth Daily Commercial (Leavenworth, Kansas) **4 Oct 1874.** I saw one of those desperadoes get a nice dose of quiet courage and stern will at this time, 1867. I had had occasion to go down the road, and had to wait for the train. My abiding place was one of those dining tents, where I had taken a meal in the meantime. Among the several persons seated around, one evidently was very raw.

His dress was semi-clerical, and as he held forth in no constrained manner about "the terrible sin" and "Babylonish Cheyenne." The oldtimers within hearing enjoyed, in an uncouth way, poking small chaff at him. In the midst of one of his tirades against "this sink-hole of perdition" a man came into the tent, walked up to the bar and demanded a drink. It seems for some reason he had been refused before. Suddenly throwing his hand under his coat he drew a six-shooter, and half-facing the crowd and the bar keeper, he said: "By G__ , I'm going to have a drink right here, or I'll turn loose!" (meaning to shoot).

To tell the truth, most of those terrible old-timers broke for the door, the bar-keeper sunk under the counter, and death to some one seemed imminent. I confess to a cold sensation down my back, and thought of several debts that different parties owed me, and wondered if I should ever be paid; the green field in which I had sported as a child rose before me vividly; I remembered one Sunday, having played off sick. I went down to the foot of Mill street and went swimming. I felt sorry for the Frogtown boy who licked me once; but what a sight. That parson, his tall, slim form seems to grow taller as, in a quiet way, he strides up to the death-dealing cubs with the pistol. He wrenches that weapon from this terror; grasps him by the throat, fairly lifting him from his feet, his protruding tongue and blackening face shows the powerful grip of the parson's hand, and, to make the picture complete, says in ordinary tones, "My friend, I have observed you before today trouble the landlord of this tavern; I am of opinion that you are entirely out of place. The landlord appears to think you have had a sufficiency of intoxicating liquor. Now observe, if you create any further disturbance, I will jerk the gullet out of you. And he literally threw him headlong out of the door. Subsequently the parson held forth on the sins and iniquities of Cheyenne, and was listened to respectfully by the subdued old sinners. I was constrained to seek a favorable opportunity to ask the parson where be learned that grip. "Oh," said he, "I used to keep a tavern down East, that's where I got my hand in."

*The first fact that strikes the truth seeker, is the extreme diffi-
culty of gathering any facts at all.*

-Letter from Wyoming Territory, 1875,

The *York Daily* (York, Pennsylvania) 12 Mar 1875. — Dr. Holland,
writing in Scribner's for March, quotes several phrases from a recent
letter from Wyoming upon the working of woman suffrage in that
Territory. It is said that the women there generally vote as their husbands do, except in cases where candidates are of notoriously bad
character, and in that case the vote of the respectable women is offset
to a considerable degree by that of the disreputable classes. The results of an election, according to this account, are not materially
affected by conceding woman's right to vote. — These facts — if
facts they are — do not of course touch the question of the justice or
injustice of excluding women from the right of suffrage, but they influence what in general is accepted as more account than questions of
right, the policy extending the right of suffrage.

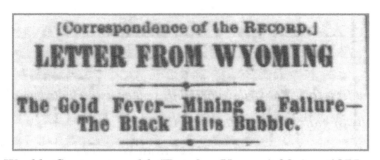

[Correspondence of the RECORD.]

LETTER FROM WYOMING

The Gold Fever—Mining a Failure— The Black Hills Bubble.

The *Weekly Commonwealth* (Topeka, Kansas) 28 Apr 1875. — Editor Record: There is no excitement, in these days when the thirst for gain overcomes all other feeling, like that caused by the discovery of gold. No matter in what inaccessible place it may be found, or the perils or hardships that must be endured to reach the scene of discovery, or chances of finding anything when they get there. Thousands leave their homes and good positions, in what is generally a fruitless search after riches. Instead of waiting until the riches of the mines is an established fact, each one seems to fear that he may be too late and rushes forth with frantic speed at the first note of excitement and in nine cases out of every ten returns on foot or drags out a miserable existence in the mines in the vain hope that their luck will come next. How many of the thousands who flocked to California in forty-nine returned enriched by the fruits of their labors? But very few, and to-day not a mining camp in the far west but what has its old California miners and as a class they are the poorest and most worthless set of men that it has been my fortune to meet. They have so long worked and waited for that "lack" they are doomed never to realise, that their spirits, once so elate and confident, are broken within them and their only care is for the present meals, not caring what tomorrow may bring forth.

Ten years after the California gold fever raged so furiously, Colorado became the subject of a similar excitement, but this was more generally felt than the previous one. It resulted the same, for while a few made fortunes, others lost their all, and are roaming aimlessly through the west, lamenting over the tardy favors of the fickle goddess. Since then Montana, Nevada, Idaho, Utah and Arizona have each had their day, and at last, through her Black Hills, Wyoming appears upon the stage. That this may prove more fruitful in yielding up its buried treasures, than were its predecessors we have no reason to believe, while there is every reason to doubt its turning out as well. But gold has been discovered and the tale has been told and how nothing is talked about but the Black Hills, and although strictly against the direct orders of the Government, as the land yet belongs to the Indians, parties are preparing to start, or have started from all parts of the country. Each party anxious to be first on the ground, fearing that otherwise the best ground may be taken and they left out in the cold.

There may be some of the readers of the RECORD who intend to try their fortune in the Black Hills. For the consideration of such is this letter written. I have witnessed many such excitement and have noted the results and my advice is this. Do not rashly give up your home comforts for a life in the mines. There is no need to be impatient as there can be but little done this season and by next, the paying qualities of the mines will have been demonstrated, when it will be time enough to go, and a way of communication will be opened. Now the country is full of hostile Indians who will dearly avenge this trespass on their hunting grounds. The route to the Hills, lays through a barren, desolate country. Bad lands, the very name of which, from the deeds of atrocity that have been committed in them may well strike terror to the bravest heart. Your supplies must be taken through on pack animals, which necessitates either a very scanty supply of the necessaries of life, or so large a number of animals.

Taking all these into consideration, are the chances worth the risk and hardships, the privations and the expense? I believe your good sense will answer the question for the present and leave the future to decide the rest.

E. S. LOWE.

Arizona Weekly Citizen (Tucson, Arizona) 24 Jul 1875. — LIEUT. S. O'CONNOR, of the Twenty-third Infantry, well and favorably known to nearly every body in this part of Arizona is stationed at Fort Fred Steele in Wyoming. In letter to us of Jul" 10, he says he intends to return to Arizona the coming winter with at least 1000 sheep. This is a very fine compliment to Arizona, for in the course of his service in Army. Lieut. Conner has been stationed in nearly all the Territories and Western States, and evidently chooses Arizona for stock-growing from his personal observation. We trust he will have success, and do not doubt but he will.

Lieut. O'Connor's post is nearest to the Black Hills wherein gold is said to have been discovered, and he says that they are in much doubt there about gold having been found in any considerable quantities in the Hills, and thinks people of Arizona ought to stand by what they have rather than take chances up that way. We say there is abundance of placer gold in our Santa Rita mountains, and the assertion is backed up by men washing out several ounces per day; the same kind of proof would be clear in Wyoming, if the Black Hills contain diggings worth going to.

Woman Suffrage In Wyoming.
[Cheyenne Letter to Cincinnati Commercial.]

Lamoille Newsdealer (Hyde Park, Vermont) 15 Sep 1875. — The practical operations of woman suffrage in this territory have always interested me, and I have embraced frequent opportunities in passing through to gather what facts I could on the subject. The system is such a fraud in Utah that I doubt whether any Gentile from there is an impartial judge of it anywhere, and shall, therefore, content myself with pre-renting a mass of evidence I have collected on this and preceding visits to Wyoming, with no comments of my own.

The first fact that strikes the truth seeker, is the extreme difficulty of gathering any facts at all. In thia part of the country is the peculiarity of Wyoming so little talked of as in Wyoming. The papers are silent on it for the most part, and politicians seem by common consent to have dropped it. I sought the secretary of the territory, but he pleaded that he had only been here six months, and knew nothing about it. The principal news dealer had only been here a year; his wife never voted, and he could tell me nothing. Several others were in the same fix, and I only found two persons who would talk freely and decidedly on the matter. Mrs. Esther Morris of Laramie, and Mrs. A. B. Post of this city, both ardent suffragists. To Judge Fisher of this city, and Territorial Librarian Slaughter, I am indebted for some facts.

We have often heard in the East that woman suffrage had worked the regeneration of Wyoming, abolishing all saloons and social evils, and all that sort of thing; but you can see without getting out of the cars that that is all nonsense. But I think we should assume in starting that the system here is no test whatever, either for or against, as to what it would produce in the East, for not only is there no extended government here, as there, but there are so few to be governed that one can really determine very little about it. Wyoming is twice the size of Pennsylvania, and has only half the population of an average county in Ohio; and of that half only one-tenth is made up of women of voting age. Obviously, under the most favorable circumstances, civil government could have no such extended functions as in the States. All officers of importance are appointed at Washington the governor, secretary, district judges, marshal, commissioners and some others. Of the 98,000 square miles in the territory but the twelfth part, lie as low as 4000 feet above the sea level, and the largest town contains no more than 2500 people.

The whole area is divided into five counties each extending across the territory from north to south; the seat of government for each is in the south end. There are five trading towns along the railroad, and in all the rest of the country the sparse population is scattered in mining, hunting and herding camps. From any town a criminal can take a horse and be in a trackless wilderness in three hours. When captured, jails are few and far between courts are often many days travel two the expense of a trial enormous. Obviously civil government cannot have the functions it has in an old state, with farm joining farm and settlement contiguous to settlement, and every county traversed by thought-speeding lines of wire and rail. Obviously each isolated settlement must be to a great extent a law unto itself; and general laws apply only in these five towns and vicinity. Elsewhere, when a criminal is captured he either is hanged or shot, or soundly whipped, according to the magnitude of his crime; for a whole camp cannot come two or, three hundred miles to two or three trials. The only places where voting and lawmaking can have any effect at all are these and Sweetwater mining districts; and all these combined contain about the children, men and one thousand women.

The entire number of women eligible voters in Wyoming is reported all the way from 1100 to 1500. I think the latter number entirely too great, but accept it as the basis of my notes. Women suffrage in Springfield, O., would be a much fairer test than here, for

Springfield has a population equal to that of Wyoming, and one-half females. The social and moral statistics of this territory may throw a side light on the question. The total white population is set at 18,000. Of these, 1100 children are in school, and it is estimated that there is enough out of school to make the entire number under majority 2000. This leaves 16,000 adults. Placing the women at the largest number claimed, this leaves 14,500 adult males, ten men to one woman. To suppose that this little handful could work a moral revolution by their votes, in a wild mountainous country twice the size of Pennsylvania, is to credit them with superhuman powers. But there are other figures to subtract.

From the police reports I learn that Cheyenne contains thirty-five saloons and forty-five prostitutes. Some place the latter much higher; but I only include those openly as such as leaving out the "suspected." Laramie has twenty-six saloons and twenty-five prosti-tutes. This includes all beer-jerkers, variety girls, etc. But as the law has pressed more severely on such houses in Laramie, it is said there is a much larger number of "kept women," not publicly recognized. At Evanston there are eight saloons and twelve prostitutes. This does not include the "suspected" and 'private,' or the few polygamous wives of the Mormons there. At Sweetwater, Hilliard, Fort Laramie, Rawlins, the proportion is said to be smaller; but out on the road to the Black hills a tent town has sprung up inhabited entirely by saloon-keepers and their "women." To sum up, the figures show the whole Territory to contain, at the lowest calculation, one hundred saloons and three hundred prostitutes. This includes one-fifth of the female voters in the last class, and gives one saloon to a hundred and eighty inhabitants. Lest the reader should hastily conclude Wyoming to be a bad country, I will state that Salt Lake City, with only a little greater population, contains at least an equal number of the "social evils." Good and evil are strangely mingled in the territories, and Wyoming has some of the finest society in America. Such being the social statistics, what effect has woman suffrage had?

First it has certainly had no particular or permanent effect in regard to office holding. When first adopted one woman was elected superintendent of public instruction, and another appointed justice of the peace. That ends the list. No woman has been chosen or nominated for delegate, councilman, representative, police judge, or to any clerical office. The offices are held by men just the same as before, and as far as I can learn most women would rather vote for men than women.

Second — in the courts it made a wonderful change, for a year or so women served on both grand and petit juries, and we were promised a renovation of society in consequence of their fine moral sense and strictness in enforcing the law. Nobody has anything to say about it now, but it seems reasonable to conclude that, if the system had worked well, it would not have been abandoned in a year or two and never revived. One man only I found who would talk freely on this point. He was an enthusiastic epicenist (believer in "no sex in politics") and served in one jury with five ladies. The testimony was of a nature peculiarly disagreeable to ladies, and from long sitting two of them got nervous and sick. The jury had to be locked up seven hours. From natural causes this was very embarrassing; the ladies were very sick by the time a verdict was found, and the whole matter so horribly inconvenient that my informant declared he would fly the territory rather than sit on a jury with women again. He still believed in women juries, but only in certain cases, where women are on trial, and their jury all women; think it would have been right to try Mrs. before a jury of women, etc. Another epicenist, a gentleman who has had experience in selecting jurors, explains the failure to get more women jurors by the fact that there are so few eligible women. The territory only contains 1500 women old enough, and of these the fol-lowing classes must be exempt, from the nature of the case — all nursing mothers, all pregnant women, all with sick or very young children demanding their care, all delicate, nervous, or hysterical women, all of notoriously bad character, and all who would be ex-empt for the same reason as men. In any country this would exclude nineteen out of every twenty; in fact it leaves only the perfectly healthy unmarried women, and those married who have no children or are old enough to have a family grow up. There is not one unmarried woman in a hundred who would sit on a jury if she could help it, and in this country, not more than one criminal case in ten is fit for an un-married woman to hear. My informant says there are less than two hundred ladies in all Wyoming who are at once eligible and fit for jury duty. This, with many other reasons of a delicate nature, had caused woman juries to be silently discontinued as utterly impracticable in the present state of society. In an old country, where there are as many women as men, very few of them bad, and a large proportion widows and married ladies with grown-up children, it might work better. For the present we have probably heard the least of women juries in Wyoming.

Third — it has made no noticeable difference in public morals though some insist that it has. Mrs. Post and Mrs. Arnold, leading suffrage ladies in Cheyenne both insist there has seen a marked improvement in direct consequence of woman suffrage. Others say not. I can only present my own observation. I was here in 1868, before society, government, or anything else was organized, and found it a rough country. I visited all the towns again in 1869, after the vigilantes hanged the cut-throats and run off the thieves, and government was organized, and found it a tolerably peaceful country. If there has been any noticeable improvement since 1870, when the women began to vote, I fail to see it, but am willing to take their word for it.

Fourth — At the polls it certainly has had one good effect to produce better order. The ladies usually come in a carriage, making a sort of gala day of it, and pass through the crowd, which treats them with the utmost respect, in fact, one simply sees there what one sees everywhere in America when ladies are present a decent respect, for them. There have been a few fights about ladies being challenged. The first young lady who was challenged at Laramie dropped her ballot and began to cry, upon which her escort whaled away at the man who challenged her vote, and sent him into the ditch! After this had occurred a few times no more ladies votes were challenged, and in that respect they have the advantage of men.

Fifth — Another marked effect had been to vastly increase the cost of running for office. It seems the ladies may be divided into three classes — a small number of the rather reserved, who never vote under any circumstances; a larger class who vote or do not vote, just as it happens, or just as they may be solicited. The candidates must see to getting these out, and carriage hire is awful. In fact, so great grew this evil, and so much was it becoming a matter of money, that the ladies, a few weeks ago, in full convention, protested against it, and declared they would walk to the polls or not go at all. The ladies vote rather irregularly, voting at general elections and neglecting the local or special elections. At the election, last year, for delegate, at least three-fourths of the women in the territory voted at the municipal election in December, probably not one in ten.

Sixth — As to its effect on the ladies themselves, there are almost as many opinions as there are people in Wyoming. Most probably it has had no effect at all, as, even did the suffrage possess some mysterious, innate power of improvement, it has not been established here long enough to produce noticeable effect. The women who come to the territories, in ninety-nine cases out of a hundred, have their characters fixed for good or evil before they arrive; they are generally of decided characters and firm convictions, and it does not seem probable that wielding so small a mite of political power could affect them either way. The political power of prostitutes, which some have dreaded, does not seem to be an imminent fact. They only constitute one-fifth of the voting women, and a candidate who should bid openly for their support would certainly lose more than be would gain. Besides, women of that class are, as a rule, utterly without any logical comprehension of how political or municipal questions would affect them, and totally lacking in the faculty of organization. Social cohesion is probably less among them than any other class of people; and a thousand of them thrown together in convention could not organize in twenty-five years. As a rule, they vote for or with their personal friends, as do hundreds of good women, and thus their vote is divided very much as that of any other class. There is no law to license them here, but the same remit is attained by fining them once a month, it being understood that if they cause no disorder, they are not to be troubled till the next month.

Nor have there been those family disturbances which some anticipated. At least ninety-nine times out of a hundred, man and wife are of the same politics. It is in this as in many other things; a low, brutal man coerces his wife by violence; a high-toned and honerable man, who disdains to usurp authority over his wife, does, in fact, govern her ten-fold more effectually by the constraint of affection. Every one must have observed that the honorable and generous man really governs his wife (viragoes always excepted) far more than the domestic tyrant, for the former is an empire over the soul and mind as well as the body. A great fool as well as a great brute must that man be who cannot restrain a wife far more effectually than by using force. The abused wife may swindle her husband in the ballot, as in a hundred other ways, but the woman whose husband refuses the claim of power, votes with him almost universally. The exceptions are said to balance about equally between parties, and exist without trouble. Mrs. A. B. Post is an active republican, her husband a democrat; Mrs. Arnold is a democrat, her husband a republican, while the late Justice Esther Morris is a moderate democrat. Judge Fisher thinks the system has resulted in a republican gain; others think just the opposite. The Legislature which passed this law — the first that sat — was unanimously democratic; but a democratic Legislature subsequently repealed it, and the governor's veto of the repeal was barely saved by the vote of the republicans in the council. So, honors are easy between the two parties.

One other fact is evident: there is a strong tendency among the mass of ladies who qualify, drop the thing, and say no more about it, and it requires all the energy of the few female politicians to bring them up the voting point. Another curious fact is that soldiers and officers cannot vote, but their wives and the laundresses attached to the regiments can, after remaining long enough. The law prescribes that persons "enrolled is the military service" cannot acquire a residence by any length of time in the territory in such service; but the ladies attached to the camp, not being "enrolled in military service," come within the law and vote at the nearest precinct. Thus it happens that a military post in Wyoming is represented entirely by its petticoats, and a very good representation, too, being neat but not gaudy, nice, rich and costly. In conclusion, I think it safe to say that the system has equally disappointed friends and foes — neither the good nor the evil predicted having resulted. And, from the evidence obtained, I am forced to the same conclusion with an old friend, who has been here ever since the town was laid out: "Woman suffrage in Wyoming has resulted in making everything just as it was before, only a little more so."

LETTER FROM WYOMING TERRI-TORY.

Idaho Semi-Weekly World (Idaho City, Idaho) 14 Dec 1875. — Mr. H. H. Knapp, of Craft's store, has received a letter from Mr. T. Savage, who left here last fall for the Black Hills. The letter is dated Centennial, Wyoming Territory, Dec 3, 1875, and Mr. Knapp kindly permits us to make the following extracts: I have just returned from Colorado all right, after a three months trip. The weather is very cold here at present, and we have about a foot of snow, it is not drifted; but a great part of the plains are bare, the snow having blown off.

The Black Hills are all the go here. I have seen fifty men or more from there and they all report the mines good and say they will go back in the Spring. A great many have gold, varying from one to two hundred dollars, which they made while there. I think of going in

February if I don't go back to Colorado. I shall work here until that time. The Colorado mines are much better than the Idaho mines are now. There is plenty of water for four months in the year. Wages are from $3.50 to $4.50 per day, of ten hours, and claim owners are making something. There is no good mining done in the country that I have seen in my trip through the mines, a distance of three hundred miles. I worked twenty days in one place for wages, and I know that I am not mistaken. I send you a few rubies that I got while working at Breckenridge, Colorado, thinking that they may be of interest to you.

From the Black Hills.

According to the morning newspaper at Sioux City, John McGie, of that place has received a letter from Cheyenne, Wyoming, which states that a party by the name of Sanders had just returned from the Hills, bringing back with him about $100 in gold, which he dug himself with much difficulty and without the necessary facilities for doing the work in a paying manner. Mr. Sanders is a resident of Cheyenne, and is firm in the belief that there "is lots of gold in the Black Hills." It seems to be the opinion of the Cheyenne people that another spring will witness such a rush to the gold fields of Dakota as has never been equaled in the history of the country.

Press and Daily Dakotaian (Yankton, South Dakota) 13 Nov 1875.

In a punning way, as well as stating it as a fact, I can truthfully say that the lightning literally plays "thunder up" there with everything during summer. It darts about ad libitum with a recklessness and facility calculated to stir the "true inwardness" of the stoutest man, and make him wish he was in a frozen zone with his mother. Nature's artillery is what keeps the noble red man out of the Hills in summer.

-Letter from Wyoming Territory, 1876.

On the 30th ult., an old man died in Atlantic City, Wy., and a Rev. Mr. Buck delivered the funeral sermon, for which he received $5, and within fifteen minutes from the close of the sermon I saw him in a saloon playing poker with the $5. That evening, he was $960 winner. The people here think Buck a mighty fine man.—Letter from Wyoming.

The *Indianapolis News* (Indianapolis, Indiana) 10 Jan 1876.

CHEYENNE.

Letter from an Old Citizen of Leavenworth.

Interesting Items in Regard to the Black Hills Country.

Good Advice to Those who Contemplate Going There.

CHEYENNE, March 29, 1876.

The Leavenworth Weekly Times (Leavenworth, Leavenworth, Kansas) 6 Apr 1876. — EDITOR TIMES: I have just returned from a pleasant visit to the metropolis of the Missouri Valley. Having spent nearly twenty years in Leavenworth, I find that since I left (a little over a year ago) she has been

FIRMLY HOLDING HER OWN

with all competitors. There seems to be no widespread feeling of distrust as to her future prosperity, but a settled conviction in the minds of her best citizens that she will go ahead, which encourages the belief that she is in a far more prosperous and stable condition than she has been for several years past.

THE BOUNTIFUL CROPS

of last year have encouraged trade in various ways. The enterprise displayed in manufacturing and the certain extension of the Narrow Gauge railway will do more to make Leavenworth what she ought to be than anything else. I rejoice in the good feeling prevailing in business circles, and hope the business men, by directing their energies to

MANUFACTURING ENTERPRISES

will make Leavenworth the city of stability and progress and the first of importance in the West. I commenced this letter ostensibly for the purpose of saying a word to those of your people contemplating a change of base to

THE NEW ELDORADO.

While our people here are aware of the existence of gold in the Black Hills, yet the opportunity of prospecting, in order to ascertain its presence in paying quantities, has not arrived. Ever since the 10th of February,

GOLD SEEKERS AND ADVENTURERS,

have been leaving this city for the Hills from 50 to 150 per day, and the cry is still they come, and off they go. The city is literally alive with these people, and the fact is nine out of every ten of those who come here, have only sufficient funds to purchase a scanty supply, and when they arrive at their destination, they encounter bad weather, snow and ice, practically putting a quietus upon prospecting, and they find themselves in a strange country, among strangers, destitute, and in a much more

---

DEPLORABLE CONDITION

than a stranded lobster. Hundreds will return, disgusted, in consequence. I would simply say to all thinking of going there to keep cool, go slow, be patient, and wait till the weather is sufficiently warm to exempt you from privation and hardship on the way, and when you get there you can work to advantage, and demonstrate, practically, by "hard licks," whether gold is there or not. You need not expect to pick up gold bricks on the surface, or gather nuggets from the trees, but you'll have to dig for it. Don't indulge in profitless golden dreams, or build any fanciful "castles in the air," but go there bent upon making money by hard work.

THE BLACK HILLS COUNTRY

is undoubtedly a rich one in many respects. Its soil is exceedingly fertile. It possesses inexhaustible fields of magnificent pine, an abundance of pure water, while its surface is covered with grasses of wonderful nutriment and richness. On account of the vast mineral deposits, I will mention a fact that has not been referred to before, which may be a serious obstacle to the timid ones, namely:

THUNDER AND LIGHTNING.

In a punning way, as well as stating it as a fact, I can truthfully say that the lightning literally plays "thunder up" there with everything during summer. It darts about *ad libitum* with a recklessness and facility calculated to stir the "true inwardness" of the stoutest man, and make him wish he was in a frozen zone with his mother. Nature's artillery is what keeps the noble red man out of the Hills in summer.

CHEYENNE

is populous, noisy, thrifty, bustling, and enterprising. Business of all kinds is good, and building progressing with masterly activity. So far as outfitting for the Hills is concerned, Cheyenne is ahead of all competitors. Everything, from a box of matches to a bellows, can be purchased here at Omaha prices. As I said before, those who want to visit the Hills, had better, by all means, wait till the weather is favorable. I met an old friend, J. B. Kitchen, here, a few days ago, who was on his way to visit a sick brother. Mr. K. is conducting a profitable business at Evanston, Wyoming, but, like everybody who ever lived in Leavenworth, prefers that to any other place.

H.C.K.

A Choctaw Wedding.

The *Abbeville Press & Banner* (Abbeville, South Carolina) 26 Jul 1876. — Cheyenne (Wyoming) letter says, describing an Indian wedding: On the day appointed for the wedding the bridegroom arrives on a pony, and leading another that has a side-saddle for the bride. On arriving at the house, without dismounting, he fastens her pony to the fence, and then rides off a short distance in the direction they are to go. Presently the bride steps out, dressed in the height of fashion a new calico dress, a white pocket handkerchief around the neck, and a large red one tied over head and ears, and a pair of new shoes across her arm, which she puts on just before reaching the parson's. As soon as she mounts her pony the man starts on and she follows from fifty to two hundred yards behind. On arriving at the parsonage he gets off, ties his horse, and goes into the house and makes his business known. By this time the lady arrives, dismounts, secures her horse, and goes to the house, leans herself on the side of it near the door, and patiently waits until some one discovers her and bids her enter. All things being in readiness, the minister, who is usually a white missionary, motions the couple to stand up and performs the ceremony in English, which is about as intelligible to them as Greek. But when the minister stops talking they depart, leaving the poor clergyman without fee or thanks. They usually go to the husband's parents and stay about a year before attempting the arduous duties of "housekeeping." After getting married, a Choctaw, if he doesn't like the squaw, gets a divorce, which is granted on the most frivolous pretext.

Black Hills.

A gentleman of this city has just received a letter from Cheyenne, Wyoming territory, which bears date March 23rd, and in it is this intelligence: "Within the past ten days over 120 disappointed men have reached here from the Black Hills, some of them in an almost naked and starving condition. They report no gold, and a bad condition of poverty and despair existing among those now in the Hills, where the valleys are full of snow and the rivers frozen over sufficiently strong to bear teams." This letter further adds that unless the government steps in and furnishes transportation and food numbers of those who have been foolish enough to go fortune-hunting in the Hills will have their bones bleached there. Rather bad, this, for the Black Hills.—*Pioneer Press.*

Manitoba Free Press (Winnipeg, Manitoba, Canada) 8 Apr 1876.

A letter from Cheyenne, Wyoming Territory, to Messrs. Irwin, Allen & Co., cattle dealers at Kansas City, Missouri, from Mr. John Sparks, says: "Cattle are wintering well, but very few dying in this section of the country. We have had some very severe storms on stock this spring and beef is scarce and high. Some few beeves are being driven to the Black Hill mines and I think there will be a good market there this summer. I cannot say just now how many shipping cattle there will be in Wyoming this season but there will be several thousand head.

Kansas Farmer (Topeka, Kansas) 19 Apr 1876.

☞ A private letter from Wyoming Territory, dated Nov. 5, gives the following glimpse of frontier life: "We have just had quite an Indian scare. Signal fires were discovered about two hours ago, and a carrier came in and reported that it was the Sioux less than twenty miles from here. They sounded the call for the Post to collect and they have started full speed, horseback, field pieces and all. We have no idea that they are the hostile tribes and think very likely it may be the Indians from this Post coming in from their hunt; but such a rumor creates a great deal of excitement and makes us feel rather nervous."

The *St Johnsbury Caledonian*
(St. Johnsbury, Vermont) 29 Dec 1876.

The air was clear as crystal and sharp steel. It was the same Sabbath that was so cold with you. It was one the best days for viewing the grandeur of the Rocky Mountains we could have had. Long's Peak, eighty mile distant, was plainly visible, while Pike's Peak, one hundred and seventy-five miles on, to the south in Colorado, could be discerned by the naked eye.

—Letter from Wyoming, 1877.

Murdered by Indians.

The *True Northerner* (Paw Paw, Michigan) 9 Feb 1877. — letter from Cheyenne, Wyoming Territory, says: "We have news of another of those blood-curdling Indian murders committed by the Indians on Cottonwood creek, forty miles south west of Fort Laramie. Two hunters, Max McKnapf and E. T. Oliver, who had been hunting and trapping during the day, while cooking their supper were startled by the warwhoop of eight or nine Indians. McKnapf was bending over the camp fire when a ball struck him, knocking him down, but he managed to crawl into the tent, and, Oliver handing him his gun and ammunition, both determined to resist as long as life lasted. The Indians approached to within fifty yards of the tent, and, secreting themselves behind rocks and trees, began their firing, which was returned by the trappers. McKnapf, exhausting his ammunition, rose to get more, when he received a ball through the body. He cried, "Tom, fight them!" and expired. His partner, having been wounded in the hip, and seeing his chances were poor, determined to escape if possible, and, grasping his knife in one hand and rifle in the other, broke through the brush to where their mules were fastened, and, mounting one of them, rode twenty-three miles, till he reached a military camp near Phillip's ranche, on the Chugwater, where his wound was dressed. A party of soldiers returned and found the body scalped and horridly mutilated, with all of the camp equipage piled upon it. The remains were brought in and buried. McKnapf was formerly from Highland, Madison county, Ill.

A Grasshopper Story.

Cheyenne (Wyoming) Letter.]

The *Owensboro Examiner* (Owensboro, Kentucky) 23 Mar 1877.

— Two men were traveling in Kansas, last summer, and when about fifteen miles from Lindsey, on the Solomon River, the grasshoppers appeared over them in such swarms as to make it as dark as twilight. Suddenly they began setting down in swarms right where the two men were riding along on horseback. The jerky birds came down in countless millions, and all traces of vegetation disappeared as if by magic.

They covered the ground several inches deep, and suddenly seemed determined to settle on the men and horses. One of them, a man named Dan Kavanagh, was thrown to the ground by the frantic plunging of his horse, and the grasshoppers, apparently attracted by a green calico shirt which he wore, swarmed on him, and in less time than it takes to tell it, had eaten every shred of clothing from him, and, horrible to relate, began devouring him alive! His companion, a young German named Fred Keiser, had a blacksnake whip, with which he managed to fight them off and try to save poor Dan. The horse reared, fell, and rolled over with him, but he managed to regain his seat, and it was not until Kavanagh had been skinned alive, and all the muscles and flesh eaten from his breast and ribs, that Keiser gave up and galloped away. About seven miles from the scene he found a ranche, and was cared for. He was so bitten that his hands, arms, and head swelled to twice their natural size, and he lay in the greatest agony and delirium for a week. When he recovered, his horse was dead, and the ranch, men went with him to the scene of the disaster. They found nothing but the skeleton of his companion, the bones picked clean and almost buried in the mass of grasshoppers, which still covered the ground to the depth of a foot. His horse's skeleton lay near him, the voracious insects-having eaten flesh, hide, and hair. As the ranchmen own nearly a whole township in that vicinity, which they are about to sell to an English colony, they swore Keiser to secrecy in regard to the affair, gave him a horse and entire new outfit, and let him go on his way rejoicing.

Letter From Wyoming Territory.

Wyoming, Wyoming Ter.

Gibson City Courier **(Gibson City, Illinois) May 19, 1877.** —
EDITOR COURIER: Having had more requests to write to my
friends of Gibson and vicinity than will be possible for me to comply
with, I thought would avail myself of the kindly offered privilege of
your columns. We received the *COURIER*, and a welcome visitor it
was.

We arrived here safe, but a tired set you may believe. I will say
nothing of our trip, except the Sabbath sunset on the highest point on
the Union Pacific R. R., eight thousand two hundred feet above the
sea level. The air was clear as crystal and sharp steel. It was the
same Sabbath that was so cold with you. It was one of the best days
for viewing the grandeur of the Rocky Mountains we could have had.
Long's Peak, eighty mile distant, was plainly visible, while Pike's
Peak, one hundred and seventy-five miles on, to the south in Colorado, could be discerned by the naked eye. It seems marvelous to
make such statements, but such are the facts. I never expect to witness so grand a sunset again.

From Summit Station we journeyed on, and arrived at home at
ten o'clock that night; and home with me now means a Ranch in the
Laramie valley, W. T, eleven hundred miles west and thirty north of

Gibson. In it are located the famous Black Hills with their forty thousand miners, who are mining the richest gold quartz that any mining district ever produced. All the mountains abound in gold, silver, iron, copper and coal.

The same mountain chains extend through our Territory from which so much mineral is extracted in Colorado, New Mexico and Arizona to the south and Idaho, Nevada and Montana to the north and west of us; and there are just as rich mines in this Territory as in any of the above named States and Territories. There is no limit to the extent of her coal beds, which will compare favorably with Pennsylvania coal, and is sold here at six dollars per ton. But we use Pitch Pine knots for our fuel, and it is by far the best we ever burned and all it costs is the hauling, being already down and looks as if it had lain there a century.

Our mountains supply a vast treeless area, extending almost one thousand miles on each side of us, with lumber for fencing and building material, and also with coal and iron. From us our railroads get their supply of ties for two thousand miles of railroad.

The principal business here is mining and railroading. There is great wealth in the Black Hills for men of experience. Out the old saying is, "Every man to his biz," and if you have not this most necessary article you had better let milling alone. For our part we expect to mine the "Grazing Privilege" afforded us by Uncle Sam's pastures, and no taxes to pay on them.

I have been writing only of the advantage of this country; it has its disadvantages also, as well as other locations. I will speak of such as seem worst to me: We are nearly or quit isolated from society with no school and but little church privilege. Located in a valley forty by one hundred miles long, surrounded by mountain none of which are beyond our view, we have ample scope to worship God as displayed in Nature.

This is no place for a lover of society; but a man with business ability that will come here and stick, can make two dollar where he can make one in the States, at almost any business he may turn his hand to. Our cattle are in better condition than stock cattle in Ill., and have ran out all winter.

But more anon. I will try to draw pen-picture of our country, and let you decide for yourselves. For my part I am glad that I came.

X.

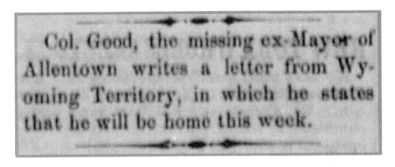

Col. Good, the missing ex-Mayor of Allentown writes a letter from Wyoming Territory, in which he states that he will be home this week.

Clearfield Republican (Clearfield, Pennsylvania) 20 Jun 1877.

OUR CORRESPONDENT with the Hayden government survey sends a breezy letter from Wyoming Territory, elsewhere printed this morning. With the thermometer in the nineties in New York it is refreshing to read about ice half an inch thick and the necessity of double blankets and buffalo robes to save one from freezing.

New York Daily Herald (New York, New York) 13 Jul 1877.

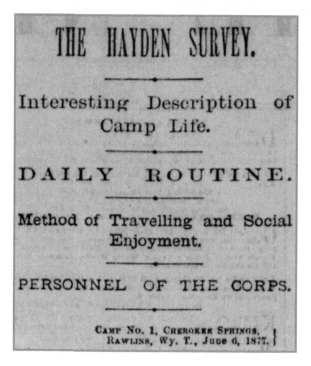

THE HAYDEN SURVEY.

Interesting Description of Camp Life.

DAILY ROUTINE.

Method of Travelling and Social Enjoyment.

PERSONNEL OF THE CORPS.

CAMP NO. 1, CHEROKEE SPRINGS, RAWLINS, Wy. T., June 6, 1877.

New York Daily Herald (New York, New York) 13 Jul 1877. — It was my intention, when writing my last letter, to have made mention of camp life on the survey, but a digression carried me so far away that my space was exhausted before I had an opportunity. We remain here for a double reason. First, in order to accurately measure a base line from which to date the triangulation to be extended northwestward, and, second, because the continued bad weather. It rains and blows, and blows and rains, with intervals of blazing sunshine. Everyone will be glad when the foundation is laid and we get fairly into the field.

Cherokee Springs gush from the foot of Cherokee Peak, a moderately high mountain, three miles west of Rawlins. The railroad company have walled in a huge cistern there and conduct the water in iron pipes to supply their needs at the station. The whole town might be included in the benefit, apparently, so far as the abundance of water is concerned. On the little stream flowing from the fountain our camp is placed under the shadow of a ragged bluff, and on the edge of a sage brush plain. Through here passes an old trail, known as: "the Cherokee trail," along which it is related, the Cherokee Indian nation passed about thirty years ago looking for a new country. They went as far West as Green River, but were not satisfied with the appearance of the land, and returned to settle in the Indian Territory. They camped for some time at these copious springs, and left their musical name as a monument of their visit. It is good circumstantial evidence.

MULES.

I have already explained that we travel with a train of pack mules, the use of wagons in the wild mountainous we are destined to traverse being out of the question us entirely impossible. There are six of us, all told, in the party, and eight pack mules only are required to carry the whole outfit of the camp. Besides this there are two extra pack mules, four mules for riding animals and two saddle horses. One of these latter is the bell horse. Mules love company, cling together and enjoy walking one behind the other in a long file. But no mule has independence of judgment enough to lead a train. On the other hand, all mules are "stuck after a horse," as the muleteers express it, and advantage is taken of this to cause them to travel steadily and to keep them together at night by having a horse to lead the march. This horse has a stock bell around his neck and is ridden by the cook, who is thus debarred from anything except steady plodding along, while the rest of us can ramble off from the train as much as we please. At night the bell horse is hobbled, and all the mules are turned loose to grass about the neighborhood, the tinkle of the bell giving us information of their whereabouts in the morning. There is no fear they will wander away from the horse unless they are stampeded, and that occurs very rarely. When the camping place is readied in the evening, the packs are removed and the cargo placed in an orderly pile, where it can be easily covered with a large piece of canvas, known as a "wagon sheet," to shield it from dew or rain; the riding animals are unsaddled and turned loose, and a few moments after, when they have cooled off a little, the leather aparejos (pack saddles) are taken off and the pack mules are free for the night. Their first move is to roll, removing the perspiration scratching their bucks, which have grown hot and irritated under the heavy packs. Then how they eat! The sun sets, twilight fades, the camp fire is replenished, and still they munch, munch at the crisp grass; the stars come out and you go in, and the last glimpse of the mules in the darkness shows them with their noses to the ground. A pack train intelligently cared for will actually grow fat upon a four or five months trip of this kind and never get a mouthful of grain the whole time.

THE KITCHEN KIT.

The first mule to be unloaded is the one bearing the kitchen kit, and while the rest are being unsaddled the cook digs a short trench and builds a fire in the hot bottom. Across this he places two iron bars, and his stove is complete. The kitchen kit consists of two boxes, two and a half feet long, one and a half feet high and a foot wide. They are invariably painted a brick red. Don't ask me why. I should reply by asking you all the street letter boxes, from Boston to San Francisco, are green. These boxes have double covers, hinged together. He places them a little distance apart and unfolds the covers backward, rests one against the other and he has a "sizable" table, eighteen inches long. His table cloth is red oilcloth. The table furniture consists of tin and iron ware, except the silver plated forks— two tined iron forks being an abuse of economy not permitted. The culinary apparatus comprised in a bake oven, two skillets, a nest of four copper pails and some small articles. All these things and a large portion of the "grub," such as salt, pepper, mustard and other small packages are carried in the red kitchen boxes, only the sacks of flour and bacon being put with the cargo.

SUPPER.

Half an hour usually suffices for the preparation of supper in decent weather, and shouted Grub Pi-i-i-lie!" is not long unanswered.
Some sit on the ground cross-legged. Some get boxes, others
bowlders,[8] others war bags, and each one takes his accustomed seat
and hands the cook his cup for coffee in less time than I take to tell it.
This is the principal meal of the day. Breakfast is over by sunrise,
and the only lunch we get is what we carry in our pockets. At night,
therefore, we feast. And what do we feast on? Why bacon, vulgarly
termed "sow belly," or very often on antelope steak, or ribs of black-
tailed deer, or perhaps beef, if we happen to be able to buy a little; but
best bacon is the standby. This is for meat. Then every meal we have
fresh wheat bread made with yeast powder and baked in the Dutch
oven, and sometimes a corn dodger or rice flapjacks. Butter there is
none, nor milk, except some condensed milk for occasional chocolate;
but you soon become accustomed to coffee without this. Coffee is the
right bower of our bill of fare. It is water and milk and whiskey and
medicine combined. Tea is "no good." And chocolate is only used to
distinguish Sunday from the rest of the week, but coffee — the best
and in the berry — is a perpetual means of comfort and strength. Potatoes and vegetables are absent, except rice and hominy, but there is
plenty of fruit sauce, currants, apricots, peaches, prunes, &c., which
being dried are very portable. For dessert there is usually nothing but

---

[8] An example of a common spelling of the time.

maple syrup, made by dissolving the sugar, and this is enough, in my opinion; but the cook once in a while indulges in a plum puff, to show what he can do, and to test the digestive powers of our hardy stomachs.

FIGHT NEAR THE MOUNTAINS.

Supper over — call it dinner if you wish — the hour or two of daylight remaining is spent in odd jobs, exploring the surrounding country, fishing, mending saddles or clothes, writing letters, putting up the little dog tents (there are four in the party, useful in wet weather, but too much of a nuisance to put up on pleasant nights) gather botanical or natural history specimens and making up the beds.

After sunset those high mountains grow rapidly cool, and a chill air from the snow banks above seems to settle down and take possession of all the warm nooks where the sunbeams have been playing during the day. Now the long-caped blue cavalry overcoats (bought in Cheyenne for $3 apiece, and just the thing for this life) are unstrapped from behind the saddles, fresh wood is piled upon the fire, the pipes are newly filled, and the circling smoke exploring the dark recesses of the tree tops over head looks down on an exceedingly contented crowd.

THE EXPLORING PARTY.

One of that comfortable six has for a whole decade been scientifically exploring these mountain ranges from New Mexico to Vancouver, and is full of the most accurate. He is our reference man

---

checking exaggerations, confirming truths which seem like exaggerations and telling strange tales of the perilous investigation of the intricate geography of the Pacific slope.

Another is a naturalist, with eyes open to all the animal life along the way, reporting the songs of the birds, finding living things in out of the way places, and making a note of every word dropped bearing upon his favorite study. He is our scientific authority and is expected to answer the hardest of conundrums impromptu.

The third member lives in New York and can descant to Western ears upon the magnificent streets and thrilling life of the metropolis until the pioneer thinks it is there the field of the adventure and danger lies and that this mountain life is tame and uneventful in comparison.

One of the packers is a miner and stock raiser who looks at every rock he sees as possibly an ore and regards "unfenced nature reaching up to our very doorsills," as only as so many ranges for un-born millions of cattle.

The other packer is a professional hunter, who dresses in beaded and fringed buckskin from crown to sole, shoots game for us and tells us stories for animals and their ways. He is "Mountain Harry" Yount, and the *HERALD* shall hear more of him. He is a character. The last of the six is an old Indian fighter, was through the Sioux war with General Crook, and endured those winter campaigns just ended, which tried the toughest of frontiersmen. His blood-curdling stories of savage cruelty are good to go to bed and dream on.

STORY TELLING.

Then, as the fragrant here glows in the pipe bowl and the darkness shuts in the fire and the little circle about from the great without, tongues are unloosed and the treasures of memory are drawn upon to enliven the hour. All these mountain men are great talkers and most of them tell a story in a very vivid way — a way purely their own, sounding barbarous to other ears, to lull of slang, quaint phrases and opportunity is it, but which is purely understood and keenly appreciated by their listeners. I heard one of the men last night tell us one of the tales of the "Arabian Nights." It is so long since I have read the "Arabian Nights" that I can hardly tell what storiess he has mixed up or how much his imagination has supplied, but you can understand that the time honored tales lost none of their interest by being told in the flickering light of a wilderness camp fire and translated into the racy idiom of the Rocky Mountains. Such are the stories they often amuse each other with; but we like best to hear and rehearse the personal adventures with which the life of these miners and frontiersmen is replete; tales of Indian warfare and ruffianism in the old days of the emigrant trail, the founding of the Mormon settlements, the track laying of the Pacific Railroad, or the gold discoveries in California, Idaho and Montana; stories of the "road agents" who infested the roads leading out of the mining regions, robbing the mails and expresses, never letting a man out of the country with any money, and the hardly preferable vigilante who for many months sought in vain to rid the mountains of these humans wolves, and learned that the persons most trusted in their councils were the ringleaders in crime. Between the road agents and the vigilantes no man was safe. The former might kill him to get him out of the way; the latter hang him on the single charge that the ruffians let him alone.

WESTERN VIGILANTES.

But one by one the vigilantes sifted out the traitors, and their murderous methods of justice at last sufficed to restore a comparative degree of order to the mining regions and give the regular forms of law, utterly dolled and powerless before, a foothold at least. The backbone of outlawry and organized violence was broken when Slade was hanged. One instance, told us by Smith last night, illustrates how the vigilante worked at Helena, M. T., perhaps the worst of all places a dozen years ago, where for weeks together you would see one or two men hanging in a certain tree behind the town slaughter house every single morning, and where there was hardly a wagon in the place that had not had a man strung up to its tongue.

At length at Helena the vigilants arrived at the dignity of a gallows, as doing the work rather more in "form," and looking more like "justice," and instructed one of their members, who was a carpenter to build it. He did so, prepared the trap, hung the noose over the beam, set the trigger and invited the committee to inspect it that evening. They told him when they got to the gallows, which they viewed as connoisseurs, that they had some persons to execute the next morning, as a sort of trial trip, and suggested that the rope was not of the right length. Eager to prove the correctness of his arrangement he went upon the platform and easily fitted the noose around his own neck. This was precisely what they wanted, but had not hoped to gain so easily. Instantly the trigger was touched the vigilant carpenter sprang into the air, and the "trial trip" was over.

Those were the days when the poet Stoddard was a schoolboy in Oregon; Bret Harte was mining in Calaveras, and Mark Twain was staging it westward and doing newspaper work in Virgina City. At that time Joaquin Miller was an express rider in Oregon. One day, when in a Portland restaurant, three men attacked him. Joaquin sprang upon a keg in the corner, drew and cocked two revolvers and drove his assailants out of the place. One of these three was Bludsoe, perhaps the original of Bret Harte's hero. Another was a young ruffian who had the reputation of being a "terror." He had killed several men, and at last scalped an infamous woman with whom he was drinking. He was put in the Penitentiary for ten years, escaped at the end of two, was recaptured, went in on the good behavior tack, joined the prison church, became boss workman &c. was pardoned out, went to Arizona, got into a fight, was shot dead. Thus I can epitomize the lives of half the characters whose ugly faces and deadly six-shooters are fast disappearing from the smiling valleys of the Pacific slope, which their desperate wickedness once made terrible.

But the storytellers gradually "weaken," the fire becomes coated with ashes, the pipes go out and are not relighted. One by one we seek our tents, and in two minutes the United States Geological Survey of the Territories is asleep.

> Night, sable goddess, from her ebony throne,
> In rayless majesty now stretches forth
> Her leaden scepter o'er a slumbering world.

BEDDING.

Almost your sole comfort, properly speaking, in camp is your bed, and you soon learn that it pays to spend much time in making it. One cold night from improper bedmaking will teach you a lesson you will remember. The proper supplies in the way of bedding consist of the following articles: — A piece of moderately heavy ducking, water-proofed, fourteen feet long by four feet wide; a buffalo robe, trimmed into a rectangular piece sufficient to lie underneath you; two pairs of thick California blankets, those costing $10 a pair being good enough; a pillow half the size of an ordinary cue, covered with tough cloth, or, as mine is, carriage oilcloth, to prevent becoming soaked in case of wetting. Air your bed in the sun thoroughly during the day. Then, before dark, spread your canvas straight out, double your blankets and lay them out smoothly on top of each other, covering one end of your canvas. After the wrinkles are all smoothed out fold your blankets lengthwise once over evenly to the edge, draw the remainder of your canvas up over the foot, thus covering the blankets completely, and your bed is made. Then you can drag it into your tent or place it wherever you want it, pulling the open edges of your blankets to leeward. Your bed is now made. You have a canvas, buffalo robe and four thicknesses of blankets under you and the same over you (except the buffalo robe), the blankets also passing full thickness behind your back. You can hold the edges tight together in front, pull the ends of the canvas over your head, if it rains, and— pleasant dreams to you. Your pillow is a great comfort. If you do not have one you must use your saddle or your boots, or a piece of wood. A warm nightcap is also a comfort, as a broad brimmed hat is hard to keep on your head during sleep. I always undress even in coldest weather, being far more refreshed than when sleeping clothed. A good plan, also, if your feet are wet or cold, is to slip on a pair of dry woollen socks when you go to bed. You can kick them off before morning if you are too warm.

SLEEP.

One's sleep in this crisp air after the fatigues of the day, is sound and serene — rarely disturbed by dreams; but in a bad country for grass you sometimes awake to find a mule standing over you, or are bereft of "tired nature's sweet restorer," by the long drawn and persistent howling of the prairie wolves (coyotes),who— I use the personal pronoun advisedly — will sneak in and chew the straps off the saddle under your head if you do not keep your eyes open.

MORNING DAWNS.

But the morning— ah! that's a time that tries men's souls! In this land a man will find it very unpleasantly cold to be with her when

— another day stands tiptoe on the misty mountain top.

You awake at daylight a little cold, readjust your blankets and want to go to sleep. The sun may put forth from the "golden window of the east" and flood the world with limpid sunshine; the stars may pale and the black of the midnight sky be diluted with light to that deep and perfect morning blue into which you gaze to unmeasured depths; and the air may become a pervading champagne, dry and delicate, every draught of which tingles the lungs and spurs the blood along the veins with the joyous speed; the landscape may stretch away in airy undulation of prairie or end is snow pointed pinnacles, lifting themselves sharply against the azure, yet sleep will claim you. The very quality of the atmosphere which contributes to all this beauty and makes it so delicious to be awake renders it equally blessed to slumber. One becomes so accustomed to sleeping in the open air that even the confinement of a flapping tent seems oppressive and the ventilation of a sheltering spruce bough is bad.

But some mornings are not in the least glorious. The rain and snow is driven hard before a mountain wind, or ice ball an inch thick must be broken before you can wash, and the icy water hurts your sunburned neck and peeling nose, and strikes like needles into the wound on your hands. I have repeatedly in bygone days got up at daylight, when the canvas over me was frozen as stiff as sheet iron, and the wind blowing a gale. A man gets into his frosty trousers with considerable celerity under those circumstances, and murmurs as he dances round in his cold boots: —

Lives there a man with soul so dead,

132

Who never to himself hath said;

"I dearly love my little bed."

Breakfast is over soon after sunrise, our munitions of peace are put upon the mules, the packing being an art only to be learned here and by six o'clock the bell horse meanders off, the mules string after him, the workers of the party diverge to their day's field of labor, and the sluggish smoke of the dying camp fire is quickly left behind.

Such is the field life of Dr. Hayden's corps.

Gibson City Courier (Gibson City, Illinois) 10 Aug 1877. — EDITOR COURIER: Some time has elapsed since I wrote you. We have to make hay here while the sun shines as well as elsewhere. The weather has been very fine for the last sixty days, and to-day at eleven o'clock I do not think that the thermometer stood at over sixty degrees — a good cool breeze blowing, the sky clear and cloudless. I am improving in health very rapidly, and enjoy the range work very well. The round up is over.

Nearly every one has taken home their stock and branded their calves and turned them out on the range to run for another year. Haying is now at hand. We start mowers in the morning; intend to cut 300 tons if we can find that much on the ranch. The river did not rise as high as usual, consequently our hay crop will be short. Our hay land consists of bottom land that is over flowed by the river in its June flood. Homer and Largent, two Boston boys that are ranching here have just closed a contract with the U. S. Government officials here for one thousand tons of hay, at $16.45 per ton. We had a bid in on same contract for $17.50 per ton, but they underbid us. They will make a nice thing but of it; but we do not anticipate any trouble selling ours at fifteen dollars, as we can sell all we will deliver in Laramie now, for twenty dollars per ton.

Laramie city is our market and is distant some seventeen miles, and I never saw better roads than we have here. The town contains 3500 inhabitants and are a wide awake class of citizens. Its buildings are very substantial, if we take into consideration that it is only seven years old. It has an iron foundry and machine shops that work three hundred men.

The Laramie Plains are fully occupied, but just as fine grazing if not better, can be found in the north part of the Territory. One of the leading advantages of the Territory is, that a man can invest all his capital in stock. His brand is his fence; Uncle Sam furnishes "the pasture and there is no danger of your cattle getting into someone's corn field.   **X.**

WAIST DEEP IN SNOW.

FROSTY MIDSUMMER ADVENTURES.

What Uncle Sam's Geological Surveyors Are Doing—Incidents of Prof. Hayden's Tour—Scaling Fremont's Peak—Glacier Lakes With Trout.

Reading Times (Reading, Pennsylvania) 24 Aug 1877. — The territories are the field of operations for Uncle Sam's Geological Surveyors. Lieut. C. A. H. McCauley is conducting one that left Fort Garland, N. M. some weeks ago and Mr. G. A. Endlich was with Prof. Hayden's exploring party in the Rocky Mountains. A recent letter from Evanston, Wyoming Territory gives the following graphic account of the scaling of Fremont's Peak by Hayden's party. The writer says:

ROLLING HILLS — LUXURIANT GRASS.

From Camp Stambaugh the party took a route along the southern base of the Wind River Mountains to the head of the Sweet Water. The entire route was found to be well timbered, and the rolling hills, which formed much of the way, were found to be luxuriantly covered with grass. The party arrived at a point near the head of the Sweet Water on the 23d of June, and encamped at the edge of an extensive forest some six or eight miles from the foot of the most abrupt portion of the range, from where arrangements were made for a side trip with a small detachment of the party, but on the following morning, the 24th of June, the snow began to fall heavily, and the attempt to make a side exploration was abandoned.

FIRST START FOR FREMONT'S PEAK.

The next morning came forth more encouragingly, the sky being clear. The party started quite early in the morning, and after some two hours' hard riding reached a point from where it was impossible to proceed further with mules. The animals were picketed, instruments unpacked and divided among the members of the small party, and at 7 A. M. they started on foot over an immense snow field for the summit of Fremont's peak, which is the highest in the southern end, if not the highest mountain in the range. After some four hours and a half of the most arduous labor, traveling over a snow field of incalculable depth and

LAKES FROZEN SOLIDLY TO THE BOTTOM,

the party reached the summit just in time to meet a heavy cloud, accompanied by a fall of snow and a violent gale of wind, with the thermometer far below freezing point. The boots of the party being frozen on their feet and Mr. Wilson, in charge of the party, came very near having one of his hands frozen, so cold was the weather. He having to carry one of the large instruments, the metal of which added much to the intensity of the cold. It was not long ere the party became convinced of the uselessness of even attempting to work, as the clouds continued to spread, and the storm became more threatening, until the points to be located from the summit of Fremont's peak were almost wholly obscured.

SECOND EFFORT — ASCENT MADE.

Under these adverse circumstances the party had to return and await a better opportunity and to return over a route already trodden with much labor and suffering is one of the most trying necessities of an explorer's experience, realizing that all this labor must be again performed in order to succeed. At the base of the peak the party remained all night only to find the next day so unsettled as to forbid another attempt. On the following day, June 27, another and successful attempt was made. The party moved their bedding as far up the mountain as it was possible to reach with a pack mule the previous evening, and from this point started on foot at 4 o'clock A. M., and reached the summit at 9 o'clock. The weather proved clear, but intensely cold, with a heavy wind. This time Mr. Wilson succeeded in obtaining the necessary observations, and when concluded the party began the descent.

WADING WAIST DEEP IN SNOW.

The journey down was comparatively easy. except on the level portions of the country where great beds of snow remained, and on which the direct rays of the sun fell, thus softening it to such a degree that the members of the party frequently went through to their waists, making the trip back quite wearisome. Mr. Wilson remarks that the quantity of snow in this range of mountains is almost incredible. Not only are the sides of the mountains covered, but all the high amphitheatres are filled, often to a depth of fifteen feet; and these basins spread over many square miles, and in many of these amphitheatres were found lakes of considerable extent, solidly frozen over, as one would only expect to find them in the dead winter scaling Fremont's peak. From this point the party marched north west along the foot hills of the range through most interesting country, well watered and abundantly supplied with grass. The streams flowing through this region are tributary to the Green river. The party then camped near the margin of a beautiful lake, at the foot of the outlying hills, at the head of New fork of Green river, where the main camp remained. From here another side journey was made to Fremont's peak, which was reached after the usual difficulties, the snow being quite deep far down below timber line.

GLACIER LAKES WITH TROUT.

This point, or one near it, is probably the one Gen. Fremont ascended some 35 years since: but as the summit was covered by a heavy drill of snow, the party could find no traces of his visit. The day was not a favorite one, yet a satisfactory series of observations were secured. Along the branches of the New fork were found some four or five very beautiful lakes, ranging from two to four miles in length, surrounded by gentle rolling hills, and skirted by groves of pine and quacking aspen, the water was clear, and large trout could be seen in schools swimming far out in the lakes. The lakes have been formed by glaciers, terminal moraines having formed great dams behind which the water has accumulated.

> Mr. A. D. Wilson, in charge of the primary triangulation party is now at work along the line of the U. P. R. R., between Rawlin's Springs and Green river, locating the principal peaks in sight of the road, and connecting his work with that of the 40th parallel by Clarence King. Mr. W. has already located all the prominent mountains north and west including Fremont's peak and the grand Tetons.

The *Red Cloud Chief* (Red Cloud, Nebraska) 13 Sep 1877.

The *New Century* (Fort Scott, Kansas,) 3 Oct 1877. — DEAR
EDITOR; Perhaps you would like to hear from Scottie. I came here
four weeks ago from Denver visiting Plattville, Evans and Greeley, en
rout. Plattville is a station on the D. P. R. R. Small place, two stores,
school house, shoemaker and a cheese factory, about fifteen families.
it is situated on the east side of the South Platte in a vast sandy plain
with very little grass but considerable weeds, they have some large
ditches that are from ten to fifteen miles that take water out of the
Platte for the purpose of irrigation, where the land is well irrigated
they raise very good wheat and barley. While at Plattville I visited
Longmont on the St. Verain creek about twenty miles east of the
mountains. There I saw the best wheat fields and the most that I ever
saw at any time; that was about the first of August and the harvest had
just commenced but there is very little land cultivated in comparison
to the extent of the country, but there are plenty of stock raisers. Evans sixteen miles down the Platte is quite a nice village of about 650
inhabitants and is the county seat of Weld county. College, school
buildings, court house, a good business and agricultural town. Greeley, four miles north of Evans, population of 2,300 very enterprising
people. They have one of the prettiest towns and the best agricultural

---

and grazing, regions in Colorado. Here they have several of the largest irrigating canals and ditches yet constructed and in successful operation. Cheyenne the county seat of Laramie county, on the U. P. It is fifty-five miles north of Greeley and halfway between Omaha and Ogden and is the largest town on the road between the two places. Population of 3,000 elevation, 6,041 feet. Watered by Crow Creek, a small mountain stream whose waters supply the town for common purposes and irrigation, very good water is obtained by digging twenty-five to thirty feet. This city has a fine court house, public - school, churches, three first-class hotels, fine hotels, fine business houses and are doing a large business with the Black Hills country. The railroads have a round house for twenty engines, also repair shop on a small scale. A railroad is being built from here to Denver by the way of Fort Collins and Longmont. I like the country around here better than around Denver, although Cheyenne is 972 feet higher than Denver they seem to have more rain and the plains look much greener.

Camp Carlin is two miles northwest of here on Crow Creek and is the great supply depot of army and Indian agencies of the north and west. It has sixteen large depots for government provisions and supplies here, also — the government shops, wagon, blacksmith and harness shops, some very nice houses for offices and barracks for the men, also stables and yards for the stock. One mile further, up the creek is Ft. D. A. Russell with fine buildings for the accommodation of sixteen companies also a large sutler's store, saloon and billiard

Hall. These are beautifully located on the bluff of Crow Creek and are well supplied with water. The prairie is high, dry and rolling, There are but few troops here now as they are nearly all in Montana looking for Joseph. There is no farming or gardening done near here, everything has to be shipped here and all fruits and vegetables are very high. We have, recently had a great temperance revival here and over four hundred have taken the pledge. Yesterday, was the election, 1471 votes were polled between, three and four were ladies, the majority of them voting the democratic ticket in the whiskey interest. I have tried to be brief but letter is already too long, will close, more anon.

Yours Respectfully
D.P.G.

GENERAL SHERMAN.

Writes About His Visit to the National Park and the Great Geysers.

The following extracts are taken from one of General Sherman's letters giving an account of his journeyings in the great wild west. He says:

I suppose you would like to hear something about

The *Watertown News* (Watertown, Wisconsin) 24 Oct 1877. —

NATIONAL PARK,

or "Woodland," as it is called here. As you know, I came from the Big Horn here with two light spring-wagons and one light wagon, with six saddle horses. Here we organized the party —Colonel R. Bacon, my son, and self; three drivers, one packer, four soldiers, and live pack-mules, making four officers, four soldiers, one citizen, and twenty animals. The packer was also guide. We had good maps by Captains Barlow and Hoop, of the engineers, which we found very accurate. Our route of travel was about twenty miles a day or less.

Our first day's travel took us southeast over the mountain range to the valley of the Yellowstone; the next two days to the month of Gardner's river. Thus far we took our carriages, and along the valley are scattered ranches, at a few of which were fields of potatoes, wheat, and oats, with cattle and horses. At the north of Gardner's river begins the park, and up to that point the road is comparatively easy and good, but here begins the real labor, nothing but a narrow trail, with mountains and ravines so sharp and steep that every prudent horseman will lead instead of riding his horse, and actual labor is hard. The first day has nothing of interest but scenery of the boldest mountain character, the highest mountains marked with snow patches, and the streams coming from the real ice water. The sun at midday had a tropic heat, while at night water freezes in the buckets, and no reasonable amount of covering will keep one warm.

There is an abundance of pine wood for fires, and the mountain passes are excellent for the animals. The next day is consumed in slowly traveling up Mount Washburn, the last thousand feet of ascent on foot. This is the summit so graphically described by Lord Dunraven in the most excellent book recently published under the title of the "Great Divide." Only his lordship assumed Mount Washburn to be the apex of this continent, which it is not; but from Mount Washburn is plainly seen, as on a map at one's feet, the whole of the National Park, and the mountains to the south of the Yellowstone lake, whence how the waters, east, west, north, and south. This, is demonstrated by Captain Barlow's map, but takes from the narration of Dunravan not a particle of interest for any man standing on Mount Washburn feels as though the whole world was below him. The view is simply sublime, with the labor of reaching it once, but not twice. I do not propose to try it again.

Descending Mount Washburn by a trail through woods, one emerges into the meadows or springs out of which Cascade Creek takes its waters, and following it to near its mouth, you camp and walk to the great falls, and the head of the Yellowstone canon. In grandeur, majesty, coloring, etc., these probably equal any on earth. The painting by Moran in the capitol is good, but painting and words are unequal to the subject. They must be seen to be appreciated and felt.

General Roe and I found a jutting rock about a mile below the Lewn Falls, from which a perfect view is had of the Lewn Falls and the canon. The upper falls are given at 125 feet, and the lower at 350. The canon is described as 2.000 feet. It is not 2,000 immediately below the Lewn Falls, but may be lower down, for this canon is thirty miles long, and when it breaks through the range, abreast of Washburn, may be 200 feet. Just below the Lewn Falls, I think 1,000 feet would be nearer the exact measurement, but it forms an actual canon, the sides being almost vertical, and no one venturing to attempt a decent. It is not so much the form of this canon, though fantastic in the extreme, that elicited my admiration, but the coloring. The soft rock through which the waters have cut away are of the most delicate colors —huff, gray, and red —all so perfectly blended as to make a picture of exquisite finish. The falls and cannon of the Yellowstone will remain to the end of time objects of natural beauty and grandeur to attract the attention of the living.

Up to this time we had seen no geysers or hot springs, but the next day, eight miles up from the falls, we came to Sulphur Mountain, a bare, naked, repulsive hill, not of large extent, at the base of which were hot, bubbling springs, with all the pond crisp with sulphur, and six miles from there, up, or south, close to the Yellowstone, we reached and camped at Mud Springs, These, also, are hot, most of them muddy. Water slushed around as in a boiling pot. Some were muddy water, and others thick mud, puffing up just like a vast pot of mush.

Below the falls, the Yellowstone is a rapid, bold current of water, so full of real speckled trout, weighing from six ounces to four and one-half pounds, that, in the language of a settler, it is no "trick" at all to catch them. They will bite at an artificial fly, or better at a live grasshopper, which abound here; but above the falls the river is quiet, flowing between low, grassy banks, and finally ending, or rather beginning, in the Yellowstone Lake, also alive with real speckled trout. Below the falls these trout are splendid eating, but above, by reason of the hot weather, some of the fish are wormy, and generally obnoxious by reason thereof, though men pretend to distinguish the good from the bad by the color of the spots. I have no hesitation in pronouncing the Yellowstone, from the Big Horn to its source, the finest trout-fishing stream on earth.

From the Mud Springs the trail was due west, crosses the mountain range, which separates the Yellowstone from the Madison, both tributaries of the Missouri; descends this tributary to the west fork of the Madison, and here is the lower geyser basin. It would require a volume to describe these geysers in detail. It must suffice now for me to say that the lower geyser basin presented a series of hot springs, or basins of water, coming up from below, hot enough to scald your hand, boil a ham, eggs, or anything else —clear as crystal, with basins of every conceivable shape, from the size of a quill to actual lakes, a hundred yards across, one feels that in a moment he may break through and be lost in a species of hell. Six miles higher up the West Madison is the Upper Geyser Basin —the spouting geyser —the real object and aim of our visit. To describe these in detail would surpass my ability, or the compass of a letter. They have been described by Lieutenant Duane, Hayden, Strong, Lord Dunraven, and many others. The maps by Major Ludlow, of the engineers, locate the several gey-sers accurately. We reached the Upper Geyser Basin at 12 noon of one day, and remained there till 4. p. m. of the next. During that time we saw the old "Faithful" perform at intervals varying from sixty-two minutes to eighty minutes.

The intervals vary, but the performance only varies with the wind and sun. The cone, or hill, is of soft, decaying lime, but imme-diately about the hole, which is irregular, about six feet across, the incrustation is handsome, so that one can look in safely when the gey-ser is at rest. So regular are its periods of activity, that we could foretell its movements within a few minutes. Sometimes we stood near enough to feel the hot spray, at others we sat at our camp, about 300 yards away. Each eruption was similar, preceded by about 5 minutes of spluttering, and then would arise a column of hot water, steaming and smoking, to the height of 125 or 130 feet, the stream go-ing a hundred or more feet higher, according to the state of the wind. It was difficult to say where the water ended, and steam began and

147

this must be the reason why different observers have represented different results. The whole performance lasts about five minutes, when the column of water gradually sinks, and the spring assumes its normal state of rest. This is but one of some twenty of the active geysers of this basin. For the time we remained, we were lucky, for we saw the Beehive in eruption; the town and grotto were repeatedly in agitation, though their jets did not rise more than twenty feet. We did not see the Giant or the Grand in eruption, but they seemed busy enough in bubbling and boiling. One is fairly brilliant by the variety, extent, and activity of these boiling and bubbling caldrons of hot water. They do not seem to me to be volcanic, but rather the result of chemical action underneath, which produces heat and gases, which give force and activity to these geysers. Externally, they are not as beautiful as the formation of some under the water, exquisite in form, but crumbling in the hand, and slaky when dry.

The specimens gathered by the curious and carried off amount to nothing. The real thing is the quantity, variety, and forms of action of these geysers. On our return trip we again visited points of most interest and some new ones, and, on approaching our wagons at the mouth of Gardner's River, we took in the mammoth spring, called Soda Mountain. This, also, is the result of hot spring or geyser action, but not comparable with the upper Geyser Basin. We got back yesterday, bringing back every horse and mule in good condition. The reason was our party was small, and we carried nothing but the smallest possible baggage and soldiers' rations only; no luxuries, no superfluities. The whole distance traveled was about 300 miles, and the time fifteen days. I would give these data as about the least time needed to see these great natural curiosities. The trip is a hard one and cannot be softened.

The United States have reserved this park, but has spent not a dollar in its care. The paths are mere Indian trails, in some places as bad as bad can be. There is a little game in the park now, we saw two bears, two elk, and about a dozen deer and antelopes, but killed none. A few sage chickens and abundance of fish completed all we got to supply our wants. The whole park is high and healthy, with abundance of good grass and water at this season. The general elevation above the sea is from 11,000 to 12,000 feet, and in winter must be simply uninhabitable and unapproachable. We found good weather, and were highly favored in every respect. In some parts the musquito and horse-fly were active, but not as bad as described before we started. We saw no signs of Indians, and felt no more a sense of danger than we do here. Some four or five years ago parties swarmed to the park from curiosity, but now the trail is very slack. Two small parties of citizens were in the park with us, and on our return we met some others, but all small.

Chapter 9: 1878

The rush and roar of the steam is heard for a long distance, the flow of the water as it is impelled far upward in a steady stream, with no apparent effort, is of the most grand and sublime character, while the sunbeams, glancing upon the magnificent and steady fountain, tint its bubbles mid spray with all of the brilliant and varying colors of the rainbow.

-Letter from Wyoming Territory, 1878.

A ROMANTIC CAREER.

Harrisburg Telegraph (Harrisburg, Pennsylvania) **31 May 1878**.
— De Rudio is the man who, with Sergeant O'Niel, had such a marvellous two days' experience in the midst of the hostile Sioux two years ago, keeping them at bay from cover with a repeating rifle for hours, then traveling through their country for two days without food or knowledge of their situation. De Rudio was originally an officer in the Austrian army, but was expelled or exiled for sympathy with the oppressed Italians. On the 10th of January, 1858, De Rudio dropped into Paris. He was a fellow - conspirator of Felice Orsini. It was planned that the Emperor should die at one of his grand balls at the hand of a guest's dagger. De Rudio said: "Kill him when he is surrounded by his lancers in the public street, when he has every guard thrown around his imperial person!" The plot was changed, and the

150

now historical scene of January 14, 1858, followed. De Rudio's book gives a picture of the drama in front of the Grand Opera House that is remarkably distinct. There were five hand-grenades, or bombshells, to be thrown, three into the royal carriage and one some distance in front and one in the rear to keep back the crowd until the conspirators were sure of their work and escape. The Emperor's carriage, with the Emperor and Empress Eugenie in it, approached the grand stairway of the opera house through a file of lancers on either side. De Rudio says he was standing immediately behind the soldiers when the carriage came up, watching the conspirator who was commissioned to throw the first grenade. When he saw his arm make a curve through the air, De Rudio dropped to the ground; quick as the explosion occurred he raised himself up and tossed his grenade over the heads of the lancers and again dropped, waiting for Orsini to throw the third one, but Orsini was blinded by the smoke from De Rudio's shell and wounded in the head; this miss of Orsini kept the conspirators from throwing their grenades until it was too late; one more was thrown out of its order. De Rudio's shell fell under the front wheels, killing the horses, the coachman, and tearing out the whole side of the carriage. There was the wildest dismay. It was an attack in the dark. The lancers fell back, the crowd scattered, the horses plunged to the right and left, and confusion confounded reigned supreme. De Rudio's design was to dash through the lancers and finish his majesty with a dagger if the grenades failed. Orsini's blindness prevented the execution of that part of the plot. De Rudio knew that his own life was worth nothing if he broke for the carriage before the third grenade was thrown. He therefore waited until the third explosion occurred. The delay in delivering it, and the fact that it was thrown by the fourth man instead of the third, demoralized the working of the plot and gave the lancers time to rally and surround the carriage. De Rudio saw that personal knowledge of the Emperor's death was impossible at that time. He withdrew from the scene. There had been several killed and any amount of consternation created, and our conspirator was pretty well satisfied that the object of his attack was dead. He rapidly realized that all Paris was startled, and before sunrise all France would be. It was a night of terror in the city. The extent of the conspiracy was a secret to all except the conspirators. There was universal dread of all the possibilities of a commune. During the night there were 54 killed and 117 wounded. The storm passed, and the Emperor and Empress remained unharmed. At 3 o'clock in the morning De Rudio was arrested at his lodgings. A room-mate and fellow-conspirator, Pieri, had been arrested, and, upon his relations with De Rudio, the latter was suspected and brought before the Judge of Instructions for a preliminary hearing. The plot covered that contingency, and in a few minutes De Rudio proved an alibi and was discharged. He was subsequently rearrested, sentenced to the guillotine, and his sentence was only commuted on the scaffold steps. He was then sentenced to the French penal settlement in Guinea, Africa, from which he escaped to America, where he joined the United States regular army. *Letter from Bismarck, Wyoming Territory.*

The Geysers.

Juniata Sentinel and Republican (**Mifflintown, Pennsylvania**) · **31 Jul 1878.** — The most noted Geysers in our country are situated in the Yellowstone region of the Wyoming Territory. The largest and most celebrated of these is the Giantess. This Geyser throws up a solid column of water 20 feet in diameter, to the height of 60 feet. Through this immense mass of water it shoots vertically upwards many minor jets, to the height of 285 feet, presenting a rare and splendid appearance. The eruptions occur once in every 11 hours, and last 20 minutes. Its basin is encircled by a rim or bank 10 feet high. The "Grand Geyser" is another splendid fountain that shoots up a column of water 6 feet in diameter to the height of 200 feet, while the steam ascends 1000 feet more. The eruptions occur every 32 hours and last 20 minutes; temperature of water when at rest 150 degrees.

The "Giant" has a column 2 feet in diameter, and shoots up to the height of 140 feet. This Geyser plays continually for three hours at a time. The "Beehive," so called from the shape of the mound which surrounds its basin and tube, shoots up a column 3 feet in diameter, to the height of 219 feet; it plays 15 minutes at a time.

"Old Faithful," so called from its regularity of action, sends up a column 6 feet in diameter, to the height of 150 feet. It plays regularly every hour, and the eruptions last fifteen minutes. What can be more sublime than an eruption of these wonderful springs? The rush and roar of the steam is heard for a long distance, the flow of the water as it is impelled far upward in a steady stream, with no apparent effort, is of the most grand and sublime character, while the sunbeams, glancing upon the magnificent and steady fountain, tint its bubbles mid spray with all of the brilliant and varying colors of the rainbow.

Another class of Geysers are called mud volcanos. These throw the mud and semi-liquid substance to the height of from six to a hundred feet in the air, accompanied by loud explosions. The following description of a mud Geyser is given by Mr. Langford: "About two hundred yards from this cave is a most singular phenomena which we call the Muddy Geyser. It presents a funnel-shaped orifice in the midst of a basin 150 feet in diameter, with sloping sides of clay and sand. The crater or orifice is thirty by ninety in diameter. It tapers quite uniformly to the height of about thirty feet, where the water may be seen, when the Geyser is in repose, presenting a surface of six or seven feet in breadth. The flow of this Geyser is regular every six hours. The water rises gradually, commencing to boil when about half way near the surface, and occasionally breaking forth in great violence. When the crater is filled it is expelled from it in a splashing, scattered mass, ten or fifteen feet in thickness, to the height of forty feet. The water is of a dark lead color, and deposits the substance it holds in solution in the form of minute stalagmites upon the side and top of the crater.

—A letter from Wyoming asserts that respectable women can no longer be induced to vote in that Territory. Gamblers drive the other kind to the polls in a drunken condition.

St. Louis Post-Dispatch (St. Louis, Missouri) 17 Aug 1878.

Woman-Suffrage in Wyoming.

A letter to the Philadelphia *Republic* tells that the writer, being in Wyoming, visited Cheyenne on election-day to see woman-suffrage. He relates:

"I did not see a single respectable woman at the polls. On the contrary, they were all of the lowest description,—performers in low variety-halls, waiter-girls in beer-saloons, and well-known women of the town. They were driven to the polls in open wagons by the blacklegs, gamblers, and worst characters of the town.—generally the whole outfit being pretty well under the influence of tanglefoot."

The *Courier-Journal* (Louisville, Kentucky) 15 Aug 1878.
Chicago Tribune (Chicago, Illinois) 25 Aug 1878.

Women as Voters, Office Holders, Jurymen and Politicians.

The *Wheeling Daily Intelligencer* (Wheeling, West Virginia) 23 Nov 1878. — We published in Wednesday's INTELLIGENCER a letter from Wyoming Territory to the St. Louis *Republican,* giving some detail as to the practical working of female suffrage in that Territory. As is well known, Wyoming is the only locality in the United States where women vote the same as men. The idea that led to its adoption was, first, that Wyoming being the youngest of all the States and Territories, should be progressive, and, second, to throw into politics an element to aid in counterbalancing the influence of the roughs, thieves, cut-throats and highwaymen, who then constituted a large share of the population.

According to the correspondent of the Republican the experiment of investing females with suffrage proved a sorry failure. He estimates that half the women in the city of Cheyenne have not cast a ballot since the first or second election. The politics of the Territory have not been purified by the experiment.

The correspondent of the Republican is reinforced in his statement by Capt. S. H. Winsor, of Indianapolis, who has lived several years in Wyoming, and who has been interviewed on the subject by the Indianapolis Journal. He is an educated and observant gentleman and was formerly receiver of the public land office at Cheyenne; was a resident of the territory when the woman suffrage law took effect and for several years afterwards. The substance of his views is as follows:

"I regard woman suffrage in Wyoming as an utter failure, and think it is to be regarded by the best men and women of the territory. So far as can be discovered it has accomplished no good results, while it has certainly worked, badly in many respects. For about two years after the law was passed nearly all the women in the territory used to vote, my wife among the rest. But after this experience the better class became disgusted with the operation of the law and quit voting. As an instance of how female citizenship worked in one case, I remember a jury trial where the defendant was charged with rape and murder. The jury consisted of six men and six women. After the trial had progressed about two weeks one of the women was taken sick. The trial was postponed several days on her account, but she was unable to resume her duties, and a new jury was ordered, and a new trial from the beginning. During this same trial I knew of three mechanics and hard working men whose wives were on the jury, and who in consequence of that fact had to quit work and stay at home to take care of their children. As an instance of the demoralizing influence of politics on women, I remember seeing a lady, the wife of a candidate for office, standing at the counter of a beer-saloon drinking beer with a parcel of colored men. I could mention her name, but will not. She was from Ohio, and was well educated and entirely respected, but she was so intensely interested in her husband's success that she resorted to this means of getting votes for him. I saw this same lady and a schoolteacher of Cheyenne in their buggies driving colored men and women, and even known harlots, to and from the polls. In such ways as this I regard the operation of the law as demoralizing to the women. There may be others who differ with me, but I simply give my views of several years experience of the law. I may add that my

wife, who enjoyed the elective franchise during the period of my residence in Wyoming, entirely accords with these views.

RELIGIOUS.

A Few Words from the Religious Press
of the Week—What is Said of Woman
Suffrage in Wyoming Territory, of
Theatre Going, of Francis Murphy
and His Work in New York, on the
Perennial Freshness of the Gospel,
&c.

The *Brooklyn Daily Eagle* (Brooklyn, New York) 21 Dec 1878. —
The Observer publishes an interesting letter from a Wyoming lady,
giving her observations regarding the result of woman suffrage in the
Territory. It takes the ground that woman, from her very dependence,
feels more strongly than men does her need of the protection of good
laws faithfully executed, and in her own interest and of those she
loves she naturally put her vote where it will do most good for the ac-
complishment of this end. This writer further says: I am not a
woman's rightist. We have not one in the Territory, I believe. I do
not indorse the ultra idea which its champions advocate. I do not
think women will derive any special personal benefits from it exercise, outside of their general interest, as other members of the

community in good laws and good government, but I believe the result of the experiment in Wyoming have demonstrated that woman's influence in the government of the state is just as beneficial as in the government of the family.

The brutal husband is brutal still, though his wife is his equal at the polls.

-Letter from Wyoming Territory, 1879.

A Wyoming letter-writer contradicts the reports that woman suffrage is a failure in that Territory, declaring that large numbers of women "visit the polls," and that "they are not degraded by the suffrage." It was not believed out this way that respectable women would "visit the polls," and hence the fear was, not that the suffrage would degrade the women, but that women would degrade the suffrage.

The *Placer Herald* (Rocklin, California) 15 Mar 1879.
The *Washington Standard* (Olympia, Washington) 21 Mar 1879.

Letter from Wyoming.

CHEYENNE, June 3, 1879.

Vermont Journal (Windsor, Vermont) 21 Jun 1879. — It is presumed that most of your readers know but little, and would willingly know more, of this Territory and of the vast region which lies adjacent to it of its size and boundaries they may know, but of its peculiarities? Yes, some of them are of almost world-wide notoriety. It is known that here woman votes, that she is eligible to office, and that she may sit and has sometimes sat as a juror. Well, what of it? What comes of all this? You can discover the boundary line between Kansas and Colorado as readily as between Wyoming and Colorado, and you cannot discriminate between a true woman of Cheyenne and a true woman of Denver. The difference between the two places consists in the number of the population, not in its character. So far as this experiment shows, female suffrage amounts to much less either for good or ill than was anticipated either by its friends or foes. It certainly has done no harm, either to society or to the character of woman. With ballot in her hand she is no rougher, no more masculine, than without it. As a mother, a wife, a daughter, she is wholly unchanged. In social intercourse and in the Christian church she is the same as ever and elsewhere. If by the ballot she has gained nothing, she certainly has lost nothing. But, undeniably, she has gained something, and society has gained something by giving her the ballot. Her hardships are no less. The brutal husband is brutal still, though his wife is his equal at the polls. Her domestic lot is not changed by giving her the right to vote. The qualities of her husband still enter into her life and are entailed upon her. The ballot changes neither the habits nor disposition of either party. Ballot or no ballot the risks of marriage are the same, and upon these risks largely depend the weal and woe of woman, yes, and of man too. Happiness, domestic or individual, cannot be voted. Its causes are too various, its elements are too subtle, to be reached by the ballot. But the right to vote, given to woman, even if she does not use it, is something. All her interests at least, and for the most part, all her instincts, are on the side of virtue. If she can vote, even though she doesn't, she constitutes a reserved force which is not likely to be wholly forgotten, like the silent operation of law which enforces itself without litigation and without noise. Here, ordinarily, women do not trouble themselves to vote; but when moral or educational interests come up, they do vote, and seldom fail of accomplishing what they undertake. The objection that virtuous women would be readiest to vote, and so balance, or perhaps overbalance, the better class, is not well taken. Even vicious women are not anxious to appear openly as identified with the immoral. Strongly as I have been prejudiced against it, candor compels me to admit that, in my judgment, the question of female suffrage deserves to be reconsidered. I do not think it impossible that therein a great remedial power has been overlooked.

B. M.

An Iowa Diana Creates a Sensation in Wyoming.

The *True Northerner* (Paw Paw, Michigan) 29 Aug 1879.
The *Princeton Union* (Princeton, Minnesota) 1 Oct 1879.— A letter from Hot Springs, Wyoming Territory, to the Chariton (Iowa) Leader relates the following interesting adventures of an Iowa girl in

that Western wild: One of your lady residents is, at this writing, ranked as a heroine by the natives of this wild, both whites and Indians. Miss Maggio Foreman, who came to the mountains, a few days since, to visit relatives has accomplished a feat of which few hunters can boast. Miss Foreman came to the springs, which are situated twenty-eight miles above Fort Steele, on the head waters of the North Platte, with her sister, to spend a few days in the very heart of the wild country. Mr. "Jim" Adams, a noted hunter and scout, accompanied the party as guide and general protector. Mr. Adams was, if I am rightly informed, raised in Mount Pleasant, in your State, and came West in the early days of the Union Pacific railroad. Being of an adventurous disposition, he drifted about among the military posts and Indian villages, and he is today one of the most daring and bravest scouts that ever followed a trail in the Indian country.

But my story. On Tuesday last a scout from Fort Steele came up with dispatches for a surveying party away above us in the Medicine Bow mountains. Being an old friend and chum of "Jim," the latter saddled a broncho to accompany him a few miles just for a chat. "Jim's" favorite horse was picketed in the grass near camp, and Miss Foreman remarked to her sister who is the wife of Mr. Adams' brother that the horse was such a handsome one she had a great desire to take a ride on him. Her sister replied that she had often taken a gallop on the animal, and that he was perfectly safe. The horse was brought in, and the writer saddled him and assisted Miss Foreman to mount. She galloped around the camp for awhile, and was about to dismount, when a shot was heard about 500 yards up the river, and a moment later an enormous black elk came dashing out of a ravine, with "Jim" a short distance behind in full chase. The elk was wounded, and yet able to run at great speed. The writer, in sport only, never dreaming she would undertake it, handed Miss Foreman a large army Colt's revolver, and told her to go and help catch the enormous animal. Miss Foreman took the weapon and started toward the elk, which was but a short distance away at that moment. And now began an exciting chase. The horse was thoroughly trained for such work by Mr. Adams, and, as soon as started upon the trail, dashed forward with frightful speed. Adams urged his horse forward in a vain endeavor to overtake her, but the little broncho which he bestrode was no match for his own favorite steed. The elk started for the mouth of a canon about a mile distant, through which it could reach the higher mountains. We felt greatly alarmed for Miss Foreman's safety, believing that in the excitement of the chase her horse had become unmanageable, until she was seen to fire the revolver at the elk, and then we knew she was after meat. Two, three, four shots were fired, and yet the speed of the elk was not lessened, but at the fifth shot it was observed to waver, stagger, and in a moment fall heavily to the ground. Then Miss Foreman was seen to halt and fire another shot into the animal as it lay struggling near the horse's feet.

We hitched up a wagon and drove to the scene, where we found Adams sitting upon the body of the fallen monarch of the mountains, while Miss Foreman, flushed and triumphant, stood near. When we praised her firing, Adams said: "These Iowa girls are business every time. I'm from Iowa myself, and I know a few of 'em; but she can't pack off all the praise, for there ain't another horse in the mountains could have hugged up to that elk like Billy did; eh, old boy?" And he caressed the noble animal in a most affectionate manner. We had no facilities for weighing the animal, but "Jim" says it will crowd 900 or 1,000 pounds very close. A number of Yuma Jack's band of Yute Indians, who were camped near, and who witnessed the chase, crowded around and gazed upon the heroine with stares of amazement, one of them remarking: "White squaw heap brave — ride all same like wind in storm."

Hunters in the Rocky Mountains.
[Wyoming Letter.]

The *Cincinnati Daily Star* (Cincinnati, Ohio) 29 Sep 1879. — Up near Laramie Peak there yet remains a great deal of game, such as bear, elk, deer and antelope, and this is about the right time to commence hunting. There are several old hunters in that section who have their cabins in good localities, who spend a good portion of their time in hunting. They are a singular class of people and care little about life outside of the mountain ranges. As a general thing they are gaunt and wiry men, excessively fond of tobacco, and the physical labor they sometimes go through almost exceeds belief. It is no joke to walk twenty or thirty miles a day up the mountain sides, where there is an abundance of fallen timber and tangled vines, in search of game — but these men do it and enjoy it. They have very little use for the young hunters that come out from the States, and who are unused to fatigue, and, as a general thing, look upon their efforts with a good deal of contempt.

If a man will go hunting with them, he is expected to keep up and do his share. Elk hunting requires resolution, and is attended with a good deal of privation, and men who engage in it must expect to undergo ranch fatigue. Besides this, when large game is killed, it requires to be taken care of, and there is the additional labor of skinning the animal and carrying the meal down the mountain sides, or returning for it, after miles and miles of hard travel, with a horse on which to carry it down to camp.

The last excursion party of the season to Wonderland, consisting of Capt. Chebourg, of the French Navy, Mounseur Desgentias, a prominent physician of France, and Lieut. Robinson, U. S. A., and escort, returned to Fort Ellis on Saturday, delighted with their trip and the grand sighs they were permitted to witness in the Yellowstone National Park. The French gentlemen are unable to express themselves very fluently in English, but as they witnessed the spouting of Old Faithful at regular intervals, and took in other remarkable phenomena of the great Wonderland, they would manifest their surprise and delight by frequent slapping of their hands.

They speak in high terms of Superintendent Norris' operations, especially of the road constructed by him around Mt. Washburn and say that but for his efforts they would not have been able to have visited the Geyser Basins so late in the season.

Bozeman Avant Courier (Bozeman, Montana) 6 Nov 1879.

Ranching on the Frontier.

Vermont Journal (Windsor, Vermont) 13 Dec 1879. — We are permitted to make the following extract from a private letter written from Wyoming Territory.

It may be interesting to you to know how I reached the ranch, and to learn something of the life which those engaged in this business lead. The day I left Cheyenne, I drove thirty miles in a wagon in the morning, and that afternoon I rode twenty miles. Next day I rode one of my horses fifty miles without stopping for dinner. On reaching the ranch, I found the only tenement upon it was a log cabin, all one room, which was used for a kitchen, bedroom and dining-room. The logs are not laid very close, for one can throw his hat through almost anywhere (exaggerating a little). The afternoon after we arrived 5.30 P. M. — I learned to shoe horses, then took supper and slept inside the cabin on a board bunk; rose next morning at daylight, 4 o'clock, then shod a horse, mended a tent and did several other little things, saddled my horse and started on a "round-up," — beef round up.

The "Outfit."

I will describe my "outfit" I have three horses of my own at $40 each: a sorrel mare, Wapse, one light bay horse, Bones by name, and a mustang I bought in Cheyenne, named Puck. When we started on the round-up I had these three and "Scate," a horse which the owner of the ranch furnished, named after a "tenderfoot" who came out for his health from the east, and who owned him. He found this country not genteel enough, and so was not received very cordially and soon returned. I have a "war-bag," i.e., a common flour sack, with one change of clothing in it, a towel, tooth and hair brush. The last was quite unnecessary, and does not belong, in a true "cow-puncher's" outfit, or to tell the truth, any of the last three. This is your "Sara-toga," and is put in the big wagon with pots, branding-irons, and everything else. I carry my bedding rolled up and tied with a rope, also deposited with pots, etc., but wrapped in a canvas sheet. This constitutes my outfit. The wagon is loaded with provisions for two weeks. It has a box on the back, in which is carried the dishes — all tin of course, and a few of the eatables. The front of the box, or rather the back, drops down and makes a little table, but this is for the cook's use and we eat on the ground. The cook, or "pot-wrastler" of course, has to cook on the ground, with much the same utensils as the darkies use when they cook in a fire-place. Our board is excellent. We have had fresh meat more than two-thirds of the time and potatoes like-wise, canned tomatoes, oatmeal, rice, tea and coffee, sugar, white and brown, always some kind of dried fruit apples or peaches, prunes or blackberries, hominy, etc. We have had no milk, except when at the ranche, and no butter but one pot from Duck Creek, which was so strong the "pot-wrastler" would not put it in the box for fear it would walk off with it. But one finds he can get along without these very well. The only trouble is that everything is fried in grease.

The "Round-up."

I will describe a day on the round-up. We rise in the morning, as soon as we can see, at a summons from the cook who has breakfast ready. You jump to your feet, roll up your bedding, wash your face in the brook and eat your breakfast. While performing this duty the "bunch" or "band" of horses is driven, by the night-herder who watches all night to see they don't stray off, into a triangle made by tying two ropes to a tree, if there is no tree, to the wagon wheels; and then you "rope," or, as they say in the East, lasso your horse to be ridden that day. This is quite an art, which I, as every one, find can be learned only in time. We saddle and go out in different directions, four or five together, — 25 or 30 are in the round-up, i.e. in the round-up in which I was; there are several round-ups in the year, but the general round-up is in the spring, about the middle of May, when there are sometimes a hundred men in the same outfit, while the territory is full of outfits; and then there is the calf round-up, in the middle of October, and another calf round-up in March. We then split up into pairs, then go alone, and drive all the cattle we can find to one common point. We go off perhaps twelve miles in every direction, and in that way take in, you see, a very large area in one day. When they are all together, men surround them, on horseback of course, to hold them close together, and then — usually the old hands or the owners or foremen ride through the bunch and find the cattle belonging to them and run them out to their covey. This is fun to you, but is fearfully hard on your horse. The bunch may have 1000 to 4000 head in it, and you have to race your horse among them and follow every motion of the steer or cow, turn this way and that, run into several cows that don't make way, and two out of three times lose the one you are after. The cows and calves are cut out first, then the "dry stock" (steers, bulls, dry cows). After all are out that they wish, the bunch is let go again and each outfit drives its covey to the next round-up place, or perhaps neighboring ranchmen keep their coveys together, and so divide the work, and then separate when they get to their ranches. These cattle (covey) have to be watched night and day so that they do not stray off or others get mixed with them. The night is divided into three watches, called "reliefs." Besides the cattle covey is the bunch of horses. They are driven in a bunch, as the cattle, from place to place, and when a man wants his horse from the bunch he ropes him. We change horses twice a day, or, rather, each ride two per day; one from breakfast until we get dinner (?), and they are driven in then to catch your horses for afternoon. Each man in the outfits usually has six, but the more horses be has the better work be can do, and the horses will be fatter, for of course they are never fed, except what little hay may be given them when they are at the ranch, when one is staked overnight; and then, if the grass is good, he is not fed. Have just got the *job* of branding 700 cattle, so must wait a little while before continuing. More anon.

BARNEY.

171

MULES AT AUCTION.

HEADQUARTERS DEPARTMENT OF THE PLATTE,
CHIEF QUARTERMASTER'S OFFICE,
OMAHA, NEBRASKA, June 30, 1870.

By direction of the Quartermaster General, the following animals, (more or less) in addition to those advertised June 10th 1870, will be sold at public auction:

AT FORT STEELE, WYOMING.

ULES, on August 2d, 1870.

AT FORT BRIDGER, WYOMING.

130 MULES, August 4th, 1870,

Sioux City Journal (Sioux City, Iowa) 9 Jul 1870.

Descending Mount Washburn by a trail through woods, one emerges into the meadows or springs out of which Cascade Creek takes its waters, and following it to near its mouth, you camp and walk to the great falls, and the head of the Yellowstone canon. In grandeur, majesty, coloring, etc., these probably equal any on earth. The painting by Moran in the capitol is good, but painting and words are unequal to the subject. They must be seen to be appreciated and felt.
-Letter from Wyoming Territory, 1877.

Coffee is the right bower of our bill of fare. It is water and milk and whiskey and medicine combined.

-Letter from Wyoming Territory, 1877.

Bear River, 44, 69
Big Horn, 16, 62, 64, 67, 68, 71,
  143, 146
Black Hills, 85, 91, 93, 103,
  108, 118, 141
Centennial, 103
Cheyenne, 13, 15, 16, 21, 24,
  54, 63, 71, 86, 87, 88, 96, 99,
  110, 114, 125, 141, 156, 157,
  161, 169
Chugstation, 5, 16
Chugwater, 115
Evanston, 44, 46, 96, 110, 135
Fort Bridger, 45, 49
Fort Fetterman, 13, 64
Fort Laramie, 96
Fremont's Peak, 64, 135
Gardner's River, 148
General Sheridan, 13
Grand Geyser, 153
Green river, 48, 138
Hot Springs, 163
Laramie, 5, 13, 16, 21, 61, 64,
  65, 67, 71, 75, 76, 81, 82, 94,

96, 99, 114, 117, 134, 141,
  165
Medicine Bow, 64, 65, 67, 71,
  163
Mud Springs, 146
New fork, 138
Old Faithful, 153
Platte, 13, 61, 64, 65, 66, 71,
  140, 163
Rawlins, 25, 26, 96, 121
Red Cloud, 13, 16, 25, 139
Soda Mountain, 148
Suffrage, 56
Sweetwater, 43, 62, 66, 68, 86,
  95, 96
tribe, 13, 43
Union Pacific Railroad, 9, 44,
  54, 66, 70
Upper Geyser Basin, 147
Washington, 13, 40, 56, 94, 160
Yellowstone, 62, 63, 67, 68,
  143, 144, 145, 146, 153, 173

The Author

Kent Brooks is the author of "Old Boston: As Wild As They Come," has worked in higher education managing Information Technology and Distance Learning departments for colleges in New Mexico, Oklahoma and Wyoming for more than 20 years.

Growing up in Springfield, Colorado, he listened to southeast Colorado stories about broomcorn, the dust bowl and cowboys of the large cattle companies. He is a long time blogger on various technology topics for his own blog KentBrooks.com as well as the local history blog Bacacountyhistory.com which covers topics about Baca County Colorado, the most southeast county in Colorado. He currently works for Casper College in Casper, Wyoming.

Made in the USA
Middletown, DE
03 July 2022

68217280R00116